INVITATION TO
RUSSIA

INVITATION TO
RUSSIA

YURI OVSIANIKOV

PHOTOGRAPHS BY GUY BOUCHET

CONRAN OCTOPUS

Front jacket: THE CHURCH OF ST JOHN, ROSTOV.
Back jacket: THE GREAT PALACE, PETRODVORETS.
Page 1: THE MARIINSKY PALACE, KIEV.
Page 2: SAMSON AND THE LION, PETRODVORETS.
Page 3: THE TRINITY GATECHURCH, KIEV.

First published in 1989 by
Conran Octopus Limited
37 Shelton Street
London WC2H 9HN

Project Editor: Cortina Butler
Designer: Kit Johnson
Copy Editor: Ann Wilson
Editorial Assistant: Rosanna Kelly
Production: Michel Blake, Jackie Kernaghan
Consultants: Julia and Robin Whitby
Illustrations: Vana Haggerty

British Library Cataloguing in Publication Data
Ovsianikov, Yuri.
   Invitation to Russia.
   1. Russia (RSFRSR). Visitors' guides
   1. Title
   914.7'04854

ISBN 1–85029–204–3

Printed and bound in Italy by Mondadori

CONTENTS

INTRODUCTION

This book is an invitation to travel to some of the cities and towns in Russia which have played a major role in the history of the nation. It is said that to know the past is to perceive the present and, though one should not base expectations of the future exclusively on the past, familiarity with Russia's cultural heritage can bring not only increased appreciation of its art and architecture but also understanding of why its people act as they do today and what tomorrow may bring. Our journey here covers thousands of kilometres through the present and hundreds of years into the past. En route, stopping occasionally to admire the view or focus on an ancient icon, sculpture or painting, we will look at palaces and cathedrals and fortresses, monasteries, churches and chapels, public buildings and town houses: in short, Russian architecture as it has developed over a thousand years.

The finest examples of the art of building perhaps reflect better than anything else the life of the period, the mores, convictions and tastes that prevailed. Behind the places go the stories and the names: we will meet extraordinary Russian princes, tsars, emperors and empresses, merciless conquerors and merchant adventurers, gifted artists, religious hermits and humble peasants. Together they form a chain that links the centuries into a single whole, to give a sweeping picture of the enormous country of Russia and its turbulent history.

The journey begins with Russia's most ancient cities. From Kiev, Novgorod and Pskov, as the old chronicles note, 'the Russian land came'. With the advent of the Varangian rulers towards the end of the so-called Dark Ages, Kiev quickly became the hub of the vast Slavic lands and as its glory grew it began to be called the capital of a

A FORMER MONASTERY BUILDING, NOW A RESTAURANT, IN THE ANCIENT WALLED PART OF NOVGOROD, THE DETINETS.

ONE OF THE WOODEN BUILDINGS IN THE MUSEUM OF FOLK ARCHITECTURE AND DOMESTIC LIFE OUTSIDE KIEV.

AN ANGEL IN ROSTOV (*above*). THE HOLY TRINITY CATHEDRAL IN ZAGORSK (*right*).

Grand Duchy. On its squares in the late tenth century Christianity was declared the state religion, and in its courts envoys from throughout Europe met. But with time the scions of the grand dukes divided up the accumulated wealth and the mighty state disintegrated into small, warring principalities. Finally, the city succumbed to the invading Tartar hordes.

Novgorod and Pskov avoided Kiev's sad fate. They came to be ruled not by princes but by the *veche* – an assembly of the city's most outstanding citizens – and were able to prevent the senseless division of the accumulated lands and wealth. And wealth there was. Both Novgorod and Pskov looked west and maintained a vigorous trade with all the major European cities. With their backs defended by impassable forests and swamps, not even the avaricious Tartars could get at them. Only in the fifteenth century, when Muscovy came into its own, were these cities subjugated.

Whatever the fate of Kiev, Novgorod and Pskov, they were the cradle of Russian literature, iconography, fresco painting and, as can be seen in the photographs in this book, of the art of building splendid, monumental churches and mighty fortresses.

Our journey takes us next to the State of Moscow and first of all to Vladimir, for it was to the principality of Vladimir-Suzdal in what was then the north-eastern corner of Russia that the political and spiritual centre of the Slavic lands shifted unexpectedly when Kiev lost its supremacy. The principality had its own flourishing schools of architecture and iconography, but sadly the thick forests of these lands could not protect them from the brutal onslaught of the Tartars in the thirteenth century, from which it took decades to begin to recover. Baty Khan's descent on Rus in 1237 is spoken of to this day as a year of terrible destruction when the smell of blood and smoke was inerradicable.

THE DOMES OF ST BASIL THE BLESSED IN MOSCOW (*top*).
ONE OF THE DOORS IN THE ART-NOUVEAU GORKI MEMORIAL MUSEUM IN MOSCOW (*above*).

THE GREAT HALL IN THE SUMMER PALACE AT PUSHKIN.

The little town of Moscow, situated at the crossroads of many trade routes, was able to recover first and it set about increasing its strength and winning allies. Thanks to cunning political, economic and ecclesiastical moves, Muscovy soon became chief among the Russian principalities and by the end of the fifteenth century it had consolidated its power over the surrounding lands and thrown off the degrading Tartar yoke. Moscow became not simply the capital of a large country but the keeper of a cultural heritage, continuing national traditions and defending national interests. Vienna, London, Madrid and Rome were eager to establish diplomatic ties and after a break of many centuries Russia once more entered on the European stage.

In the late 1960s, when Soviets began to feel a renewed interest in their history, the Muscovy towns encompassed on our journey here were dubbed the Golden Ring. And indeed they boast the greatest concentration of original churches and fortresses, striking frescos and exquisite icons, and in general everything that has contributed to national and world culture.

The third part of our journey is the shortest geographically but no less rich artistically and historically. St Petersburg/Leningrad, with the surrounding palace towns of Peterhof/Petrodvorets, Tsarskoye Selo/Pushkin and Pavlovsk, represent the final two eventful centuries of the history of the Russian Empire, which by this time stretched from the Pacific Ocean to the Baltic Sea. St Petersburg is a city unlike any other, born of a monarch's imagination and literally rising from the sea. Squares and waterfronts are lined with majestic buildings, architectural ensembles of elegant splendour, and here is the Hermitage with its unique collection of paintings by Rembrandt, Rubens, the minor Dutch artists and the French Impressionists. Here too is Dostoyevsky's cramped flat facing onto a dark courtyard, and the incomparable luxury of the emperors' and empresses' rooms at their palaces and nearby summer residences. Only the cruiser *Aurora*, riding permanently at anchor, reminds us that a new social system was born here on the banks of the Neva in 1917.

The final leg of our journey takes us south, to the mild climate of the northern and eastern shores of the Black Sea – and to the final century of the Russian Empire. Behind the natural attractions of sunshine, warm waters and mountain landscapes lies a history of military exploits and diplomatic manoeuvrings as successive rulers of Russia tried to establish a permanent foothold on the Black Sea coast. Yalta, in the hard-won Crimean peninsula, grew from a fortress to a health resort, made popular by the Russian royal family; here is their summer palace and, more famous, the final home of Anton Chekhov. Further east we come to the great port of Odessa, which developed in the nineteenth century to rival St Petersburg, its prosperity and pride revealed in the splendour of its public buildings in the town's old streets. Finally, and appropriately, we reach the immensely popular holiday resort of Sochi, set against the background of the Caucasus mountains. This nineteenth-century settlement on the site of an old fort later developed into a spa town and in its hotels, holiday apartments and sanatoria – several built in the 1930s and 1950s by government institutions and other official bodies – can be seen the successive styles of twentieth-century architecture that reflect Russia's most recent and on-going history.

THE BLACK SEA SEEN FROM MASSANDRA NEAR YALTA, THE CENTRE OF THE CRIMEAN WINE-PRODUCING REGION.

ANCIENT RUSSIA

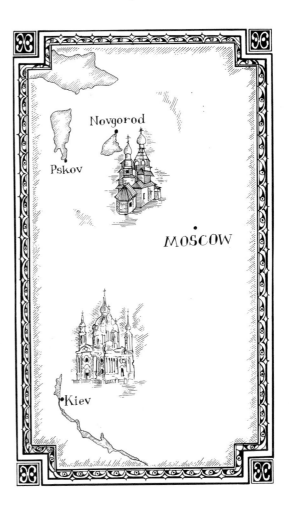

KIEV

Called 'the mother of Russian cities' and today the third largest city in the USSR, Kiev lies across the River Dnieper in the south-western state of the Ukraine. There were settlers here as far back as 4000 to 3000 B.C. but it was the Slavs in the late eighth to the early ninth century who founded a fortified town on the hilltop high above the right bank of the broad river. Strategically positioned to form the southern gateway to the Black Sea and Constantinople, Kiev flourished as a centre of trade on the main route from Europe to the East. The town quickly spread downwards to the enormous international market on the riverside, with the ruling prince and his courtiers residing in the upper city, shielded by walls and ramparts, while on the Podol or lower slope lived the merchants, sailors and craftsmen.

Ancient chronicles first mention 'the Russian land' in connection with Kiev in 852, a decade before the Northmen or Varingians, led by Askold and Dir, captured the city. The descendants of the first true prince of Kiev, Oleg, conquered the lands to the north and east, and from the late tenth century for well over 200 years, the Kievan state dominated all Russian cities and principalities. Its contact with Constantinople not only brought great trading wealth but deep cultural influences and Kiev became the birthplace and centre of Russian Christianity, based on the Greek Orthodox Church. The first church appeared in Kiev in the mid-ninth century but it was Prince Vladimir in 988 who declared Christianity the state religion and that year the whole population of Kiev was baptized in the river's waters.

The city's main street, which runs down to the Dnieper, is still called Kreshchatik, from *kreshcheniye*, meaning baptism, and, as a reminder that Kiev was the original seat of Russian Christianity, a column was raised in the early nineteenth century on the site of the mass baptism. The historic event is commemorated by the monument to the 'Baptizer of Russia', erected in 1853 on a steep slope beside the river and designed by Konstantin Thon, the favourite architect of Tsar Nikolai I, who was also responsible for the Great Kremlin Palace in Moscow. The bronze statue of Prince Vladimir, almost five metres (16½ feet) tall, gazing down on the water, is by the sculptor Pyotr Klodt, known for his horse-breaker sculptures on the four corners of the Anichkov Bridge in Leningrad.

In the early eleventh century the chronicler Titmar Merzeburgski recorded that Kiev had more than 400 churches, eight markets and an incalculable number of people. The court of Prince Yaroslav, Vladimir's son, was famed in Europe and he was related through the dynastic marriages of his children to many of Europe's royal houses: his sister Maria married Kazimir, King of Poland, and his three daughters married Harald of Norway, Henri I of

THE MONUMENT TO THE BAPTIZER OF RUSSIA OVERLOOKING THE RIVER DNIEPER (*above and right*).

France, and Andrew I of Hungary respectively. It was at Prince Yaroslav's court that the sons of the Anglo-Saxon king, Edmund Ironside, found refuge after their father's defeat by the Danes in 1016. Five decades later, when King Harold II was killed at the Battle of Hastings, his daughter Hita similarly fled to the continent and in 1074 she married Prince Vladimir Monomach, grandson of Prince Yaroslav. Their elder son Mstislav became, as was traditional, ruler of the wealthy city of Novgorod, while their younger son Georgi – Yuri Dolgoruki – became known as the founder of Moscow.

The ambitious Prince Yaroslav dreamed of making his capital the equal of Constantinople in splendour and it was he who built the majestic Cathedral of St Sophia which still dominates Kiev today, as well as numerous other churches and a new fortress wall with four stone gateways. One of the latter remains, the main, southern entrance popularly known as the Golden Gates, and attempts are being made to restore the buried ruins of the others.

From the Golden Gates the street leads straight to St Sophia, just as it did over 800 years ago. The churches of St Irina and St Georgi stood nearby but neither could compare in beauty or size to the cathedral of the great Kievan principality. Its thirteen golden domes loomed over the city and the enormous five-naved structure, occupying an area of 1472 square metres (1760 square yards), could accommodate as many as 4000 worshippers on feast days. An open, one-storeyed exterior gallery and an enclosed, two-storeyed interior gallery ran along the north, west and south sides and, in keeping with Byzantine tradition, the choir was raised, emphasizing its separateness. Here the prince and his retinue stood during services, entering through two massive towers adjoining the western wall.

Within, the walls and floors were decorated with vivid murals and tiles of sparkling smalt, and a wealth of gold, silver and bronze ornaments glittered in the reflection of hundreds of burning wax candles. The overwhelming splendour served to affirm both the greatness of God and the might of the ruler, for St Sophia was not only the spiritual but also the temporal seat of power. The choir was used by the prince to receive envoys and to hold state meetings and banquets, and the inner gallery, reached by stairways decorated with murals of musicians, circus artistes, hunting scenes and chariot races, housed the state archives and included a library and scriptorium.

Portraits of Prince Yaroslav's children can still be seen in the central nave of St Sophia, the sons on the southern wall, the daughters on the northern. Those of the Prince himself and his wife, which were on the western wall, were lost in the seventeenth century during rebuilding.

Nothing now remains of the prince's palace, which was situated in the upper city near the cathedral, although some idea of its sumptuousness can be gained from the two surviving stone reliefs that once decorated the ruler's country residence at Berestovo. One of these depicts Hercules and the lion, the other Cybele, mother of the gods, in a chariot drawn by lions. Berestovo, now part of Kiev, was then a village about four kilometres (two and a half miles) from the city, and the princes had on more than one occasion to take refuge behind the fortified walls of their palace there. Prince Vladimir Monomach built the Church of Christ the Saviour in Berestovo, where Yuri Dolgoruki was buried. The narthex of the old church still survives.

It was on two wooded hills next to the Berestovo palace that the first Russian monastery was established in the mid-eleventh century. Named the Pechersky Monastery, from the old Russian word for cave, *pechera*, it was founded by the holy man, Antony of Liubech, who retired from the world to live a life of prayer and fasting in a cave on the farther hill. Other zealots came to join him, living in the nearby caves, and when their numbers reached twelve, a monastery was formed. Antony moved from the 'Far Caves', to the 'Near Caves', on the hill closer to Berestovo, where more disciples arrived to join the network of caves and underground chapels.

As the monastery grew in numbers and influence, the Kievan princes granted the monks the hill lands and bequeathed them money to build a stone church, the Church of the Dormition, which was begun in 1073. According to an early thirteenth-century history of the monastery, the

THE GOLDEN GATES – THE ONLY REMAINING OF FOUR STONE GATEWAYS BUILT IN THE 11TH CENTURY.

THE CATHEDRAL OF ST SOPHIA: THE INTERIOR (*top left*) AND THE SOUTH SIDE (*top right*).

SOME OF ST SOPHIA'S NINETEEN CUPOLAS (*above*).

church was built as the result of the vision of Shimon, an outstanding Varingian warrior who lived in Kiev. Shimon's most treasured possession was a belt of pure gold and, in a moment of mortal danger, he had a vision that his life would be spared if a church in the name of the Virgin was built in the monastery, using his gold belt as the building's measure. Spared from death, Shimon gave his belt to the monks, who shortly afterwards were visited by master masons from Constantinople who told them that the Virgin Mary had appeared to them in a dream and commanded them to go to Kiev to build a church. Six years later, a graceful, three-naved church with a single cupola was complete; a small baptistry adjoined the north wall. It measured twenty times Shimon's belt in width, thirty times in length and fifty times in height.

In 1972 archaeologists found an inscribed ceramic slab which indicated that the entire building project had been directed by a master mason from Bulgaria. It was probably also Bulgarians who were responsible for the church's decoration, aided by Russian artisans. Broken stone slabs bearing fragments of colourful frescos and mosaics are all that now remains of the church, blown up by the Nazis during the occupation of Kiev in the Second World War.

The Pechersky Monastery became famed for its wealth and culture in the eleventh and twelfth centuries, attracting many outstanding figures, among them the chronicler Nestor, who wrote the first history of the Russian state, the celebrated icon painter Alimpy and the physician Agapit. The monastery produced smalt and had a large icon studio where, the monastery history relates, Alimpy painted many works. One at least of these has survived: a stunningly beautiful icon of the Virgin in prayer, nearly two metres (six feet) in height. It was found in this century in a storeroom at the Spassky Monastery in Yaroslavl, probably having come there from Rostov, to which it had been presented by Prince Vladimir Monomach. It is now in the

THE TWO-TIERED KOVNIR BELL TOWER (1754–1761) AND THE 17TH-CENTURY CHURCH OF THE NATIVITY OF THE VIRGIN IN THE FAR CAVES OF THE PECHERSKY MONASTERY.

collection of the Tretyakov Gallery in Moscow.

Shortly after the Church of the Dormition was consecrated, a strong wall was built around the cloister, partly to shelter the monks from the outside world but also to protect the accumulated riches of the monastery from the raids of the barbaric nomads who inhabited the steppe between the Dnieper and the Don. Stone gateways were set in the wooden wall, the main entrance on the west side, opposite the church, and the service gates on the north side. Each was topped by an exquisite little chapel, one of which was the Trinity Gatechurch. Partially rebuilt, they still survive.

Many of the monastic buildings from this time were burned to the ground in 1240, as the Tartar hordes led by Khan Batu swept through Russia, looting and destroying. That year they reached Kiev, surrounding the city and calling on its citizens to surrender. The proud Kievans refused and a fierce assault began. As one chronicler wrote: 'The creaking of countless carts, the bellowing of camels and oxen, the neighing of horses and the savage cries of the enemies barely allowed the inhabitants to hear each other speak.' The Tartars spared no one and nothing; Kiev was razed to the ground, and even two centuries later travellers would write sorrowfully of the dead city. But the Tartars had suffered terrible losses too and, bled white by their battle with the Russians, they could not risk moving any further to the west. European civilization was saved.

For the four centuries following its desolation by the Tartars, the former Kievan state came under the sway of first the Lithuanian princes and then the Polish barons. By the mid-seventeenth century, however, the Ukraine had sufficiently recovered to win its arduous fight for religious, political and economic independence, and shortly afterwards, in 1654, Kiev joined the powerful state of Muscovy, which shared the Russian Orthodox faith and offered to Kiev its only hope of protection from domination and religious persecution by neighbouring countries.

CUPOLAS OF THE CHURCH OF THE EXALTATION OF THE CROSS (1700) IN THE NEAR CAVES OF THE PECHERSKY MONASTERY.

THE TRINITY GATECHURCH: DETAILS OF THE EXTERIOR BAROQUE STUCCO WORK AND PAINTING.

BOGDAN KHMELNITSKY (*top*) WHO LED THE 17TH CENTURY REVOLT
OF THE UKRAINE AGAINST THE POLISH BARONS.
THE NEW MONUMENT TO THE UNION OF RUSSIA AND THE UKRAINE
IN 1654 (*right*); THE ARCH'S FOOT (*above*).

This period saw a flowering of culture in the Ukraine, centring on Kiev, that reached its height in the eighteenth century. The first Ukrainian institution of higher learning, the Kiev-Moghilian Collegium, was established and the printing house in the former scriptorium of the Pechersky Monastery produced many fine scholarly works, both secular and theological. Examples of its output can be seen today in the monastery printing house's Museum of Books and Book Printing of the Ukraine.

The Ukrainian renaissance also saw a building boom in Kiev. St Sophia and many old churches were restored, and new buildings erected, all in the Russian baroque style which is remarkable for its splendour. The architects of the time seemed indeed to be in competition to produce the most richly decorated building; designs were of matchless intricacy, with innumerable spiral scrolls and ornate mouldings depicting grape vines, sunflowers and field grasses. A new clergy house and a large bell tower were built alongside St Sophia, encircled by a massive stone wall with ceremonial gates. The original Pechersky Monastery church became unrecognizable under its new baroque garb: four cupolas were placed on the corners, around the large dome, and the roof adorned with small, ornate pediments; plaster covered the walls of large, flat bricks and pink and greenish-purple stones, and doorways and windows were edged with fine and intricate mouldings like stiffly starched lace.

Love of abundant ornamentation had been a hallmark of Ukrainian art and architecture through the centuries, as is clear from the dazzling display of some 15,000 jewelled pieces, dating from the sixth century B.C. to the nineteenth century, in the Museum of Historical Treasures of the Ukraine, housed in the monastery's old bakery. The many magnificent works of eighteenth-century craftsmen include mitres set with precious stones and coloured enamel, gold plates decorated with the plant motif traditional to the area, elaborate covers for Gospels and a tabernacle decorated with over twenty raised figures.

Building was particularly intensive in the Pechersky Monastery, which was given a new fortress wall with eight towers; wooden domestic buildings were replaced by ones of stone and an extensive hospital complex and residences for monks of noble birth and distinction were built. A traveller in the second half of the seventeenth century described the monks' accommodation as 'decorated with all kinds of paintings and superb images, furnished with tables, long benches, beds and stoves, the hearths having beautifully painted tiles', and he mentioned magnificent rooms containing books of great value.

THE BELL TOWER OF ST SOPHIA (1699–1706).

The monastery's new Great Bell Tower was built in the first half of the eighteenth century, after its wooden predecessor had burned down in 1718. Peter the Great sent the architect Fyodor Vasiliev from St Petersburg to Kiev to design it but he and the monks came into conflict over the proposed costs and in 1720 Vasiliev departed, taking his completed drawings with him. It was another eleven years before the German architect, Johann Gottfried Schädel, who had supervised the construction and repair of Peter the Great's palaces before falling into political disfavour under Peter II, was sent to Kiev to build the bell tower. His design was probably a modification of Vasiliev's plans for a five-tiered building of tapering diameter, using Doric, Ionic and Corinthian columns, and topped by a baroque cupola. Schädel's tower had four tiers, of significantly increased height, the first and second tiers serving as a book repository and library, the third housing the bells and the fourth an enormous chiming clock. This ornate structure, using ceramic ornamentation even for the capitals on the columns, measures nearly 30 metres (100 feet) in diameter at its base and is 96.5 metres (317 feet) high, 15 metres (50 feet) higher than the Ivan the Great Bell Tower in the Moscow Kremlin. The golden dome could be seen shining from a distance of 50 kilometres (30 miles).

The Great Bell Tower was completed in 1744 and that year the Empress Elizabeth made a state visit to Kiev, the enormous royal procession taking two months to make its way from Moscow to the Ukraine. She was welcomed enthusiastically and, in honour of the historic occasion, the empress commanded that a new church and a royal residence be built in the city. Both works were entrusted to the architect Bartolomeo Rastrelli, responsible for the construction of several royal palaces. The site chosen for the

THE CHURCH OF THE EXALTATION OF THE CROSS IN THE NEAR CAVES OF THE PECHERSKY MONASTERY.

THE 18TH-CENTURY ECONOMIC BUILDING – THE ADMINISTRATIVE OFFICES OF THE PECHERSKY MONASTERY (*top*).
THE MARIINSKY PALACE (*overleaf*).

royal residence was on the outskirts of the city on the road to the monastery. The buildings were completed in 1755, with the ground floor built of stone and the top floor of wood. The palace burned down in 1819 but was rebuilt, and today the graceful blue and cream Mariinsky Palace, standing in an old park, houses a government agency.

The new church, St Andrew, was built close to where Kiev's first royal palace and first stone church had stood, on the hill leading down to the riverside, the spot where, according to legend, the Apostle Andrew had once preached Christianity to the local pagans. The monastery that had been established there in 1086 had been demolished in the Tartar invasion of 1240 and the wooden churches built over the centuries had succumbed to fire and time. Earlier in the eighteenth century, when Peter the Great was waging war with Karl XII of Sweden, a fortress was built on the ruins of the last of the wooden churches, and now the fortress was to make way again for a place of worship.

A Moscow architect, Ivan Michurin, was sent to supervise the construction of Rastrelli's plans. A triumph of eighteenth-century Russian baroque, the church is in the shape of a four-pointed cross, shortened on the northern and southern ends, with a rounded apse forming the eastern end and the narthex forming the extended western end. The entire structure is topped by a great drum, over which is an enormous green and golden dome crowned by a bulbous cupola. From its hill setting, the church rises high into the sky, the sense of upward movement emphasized by the gleaming white of the columns, pilasters and mouldings against the turquoise blue of the walls.

At the end of the eighteenth century Paul I proclaimed Kiev the capital of a vast governor-generalship that encompassed almost all of the Ukraine east of the Dnieper. This led to a further flowering of cultural life and boosted the city's economic growth. A new city centre gradually arose west of Kreshehatik Street, starting with a broad avenue,

THE MARIINSKY PALACE: DETAILS OF THE BAROQUE FAÇADES.   THE CHURCH OF ST ANDREW (1747–1761) (*right*).

now named after the celebrated Ukrainian poet Taras Shevchenko, and followed by other new streets, which today bear the names of Lenin, Sverdlov and Polupanov. In 1837 the architect Vikenty Beretti began construction of the first building for the newly founded university; his son Alexander Beretti was responsible for Gymnasium No. 1, where the writer Mikhail Bulgakov was subsequently to study, which was followed by Vikenty Beretti building the Institute for Young Noblewomen.

The neo-Byzantine style made fashionable in St Petersburg by Nikolai I's favourite architect, Konstantin Thon, took time to reach Kiev, a provincial city where even mail from the capital arrived, with luck, in ten days. The new fashion was only taken up after a delay of two decades, through the efforts of the St Petersburg architect Strom, and it was in the neo-Byzantine style that St Vladimir, one of the largest churches in Russia, was built in 1862. The paintings for its interior were by the famous artists, Viktor

KIEV UNIVERSITY (1837–43).

THE OPERA AND BALLET HOUSE (1897–1901) (top).

Vasnetsov, Mikhail Nesterov and Mikhail Vrubel, who produced the altar masterpiece, a beautiful icon of the Mother of God.

Despite St Vladimir, the neo-Byzantine style did not take root in Kiev and other impressive buildings of the second half of the nineteenth century drew on different traditions. The City Museum of Antiquities and the Arts (now the Museum of Ukrainian Art) was modelled on an ancient Greek temple; the Polytechnical Institute was Romanesque in style, the new Kiev bank Northern Italian Gothic, while the Kiev Theatre and the Opera House followed French Renaissance traditions.

The beauty of Kiev was extolled by many nineteenth-century writers and the city is linked with some of the greatest literary figures of the Russian Empire. Alexander Pushkin and Nikolai Gogol both wrote of its beauties, and in his *Kiev Letters* Honoré de Balzac gave a vivid account of life in the city, which he knew from his relationship with Eveline Ganskaya, a rich Polish noblewoman who owned estates in the Kiev governorship. Kiev also forms the setting for two wonderful novels by Nikolai Leskov, *Pechersky Characters*, recalling the city's famous eccentrics at the beginning of the century, and *The Engraved Angel*, set in the mid-1800s when an enormous metal bridge was being built on chains across the Dnieper. The bridge is still in faithful service. A century later, in the 1950s, another remarkable bridge was built, a rivetless construction one and a half kilometres (one mile) long, named after Yevgeni Paton, the engineer who invented the electrical welding process that made it possible.

The writer Mikhail Bulgakov, known for *The Master and Margarita*, lived on Andreyevsky Street before and during the 1917 Revolution and in his novel *The White Guard* paid tribute to the lovely, historic street; his house is now a museum in honour of his memory. The imminent end of the Russian Empire was heralded in Kiev by the assassination in September 1911 of Pyotr Stolypin, chairman of the Russian Council of Ministers, whose agricultural reforms had met with particular success in the Kiev governor-generalship; he was shot dead by a secret police agent in the Kiev Theatre, before the entire audience.

After the Revolution, Kiev fell on hard times; the young industrial city of Kharkov was named the capital of the Ukraine, while the birthplace of the Russian state was demoted to the rank of an ordinary provincial city. Only in 1934 was it reinstated as the capital, when ponderous buildings were erected for the Ukrainian government and party offices; the old embankment was faced in granite and the building of a new stadium was begun.

In the terrible destruction of the Second World War, however, some forty per cent of Kiev's buildings were wiped out. The Germans entered the city on 19 October 1941 and were in occupation for 850 days before finally being driven out by a powerful surprise attack from the north and south. A memorial to the war dead stands as a reminder, together with the Victory Monument, erected in 1981 at the behest of Leonid Brezhnev, a 62-metre-high (200 feet) statue of a woman symbolizing the Motherland which towers ponderously above its surroundings.

THE VICTORY MONUMENT (*top*), OVER THE UKRANIAN MUSEUM OF THE HISTORY OF THE GREAT PATRIOTIC WAR OF 1941–45. A DETAIL OF THE MEMORIAL TO THE WAR DEAD (*below*).

Under the direction of Nikita Krushchev in the late 1950s and early 1960s, a massive rebuilding programme was put in hand in Kiev to try to solve the acute housing shortage; at the time, the average living space per person was less than five square metres (54 square feet). Rows of five- and ten-storeyed concrete shoe-boxes were quickly erected, with aesthetics being the last priority. The emphasis in the 1960s continued to be on housing, although scientific research centres, cinemas, exhibition halls and hotels began to be constructed. Kiev spread in all directions – with the Pechersky Monastery finding itself almost in the middle of the city – and eventually expanded across the river to the left, low-lying bank of the Dnieper. High-rises now stand among the ancient pines and there are even new neighbourhoods on the islands in the Dnieper – Dolobetsky, Trukhanov and Venetsiansky. There may be no architectural masterpieces in these new

regions of the Ukrainian capital but much thought has gone into creating pleasant, comfortable homes there.

In the historic parts of the city, the old lives in harmony with the new and the baroque tradition has been carried on in the restoration of its buildings, their façades decorated with colourful ceramic garlands and bas-reliefs that recall Kiev's former majesty. The ancient main street, Kreshchatik, destroyed in the war, is lined down its right side with new public buildings, fronted by a broad pavement, while on the hilly left-hand side the spacious residences are separated by green squares, with walkways on two levels connected by broad steps. In spring, Kiev's glorious chestnut trees come into blossom, to add their beauty to the sprawling modern city which stands in intricate silhouette against the sky, the shining golden domes of its ancient churches beckoning the visitor and the bronze statue of Prince Vladimir solemnly blessing wayfarers as they pass.

THE OPEN-AIR MUSEUM OF UKRAINIAN FOLK ARCHITECTURE
OUTSIDE KIEV.

NOVGOROD

(NOVGOROD THE GREAT)

Novgorod means 'new town', which supposes the existence of an old one. This was probably Staraya Ladoga, a small town on the bank of the River Volkhov near where it flows into Lake Ladoga, and which in the eighth century was a busy crossing-point on the trade route from Europe to the East. Archaeologists have discovered traces of Norman settlements and hoards of Arabian, German and English coins there. In the ninth century a new trade route was opened from the Baltic to the Black Sea and on to Constantinople, and the town shifted southwards, towards the Volkhov's sources and Lake Ilmen.

Old Kievan chronicles mention Novgorod for the first time in the entry for the year 862, when it is listed among the Russian towns ruled by the Northmen or Varingians. That year the Northmen captured Kiev, Novgorod's overlord and rival. Because of its position further south, Kiev could block the road to merchants bound for Constantinople, which caused constant friction between the two important trading centres.

Novgorod's main trade was in furs and the town attracted bold adventurers who enforced tribute from the hunters and trappers in lands far to the north and east, and whose conquests soon gave Novgorod possession of northern lands stretching from the Baltic to the Urals. Successful trade also attracted experienced sailors and boat-builders, and Novgorod multiplied in wealth.

Initially the town is thought to have consisted of three independent settlements, which came to be called 'ends'. On the west bank of the Volkhov were the Lyudin End (later known as the Potters' End), inhabited by the Baltic Slavs, and the Nerevsky End, founded by a local Finno-Ugric tribe. The Slavensky End, lying on the east bank, was settled by Slavs who had come from the banks of the Dnieper. The Prince of Novgorod lived on the west bank, on a hill surrounded by earth ramparts and a tall, oak palisade. The place was known as the Detinets, possibly from

the old Slavonic word *ditya*, which can mean child, thus a child of the rich city. And the city, thanks to its flourishing trade with Europe, was extremely rich.

Appreciating Novgorod's importance and special position, the princes of Kiev sent their elder sons to rule the town and in the second half of the tenth century Novgorod's lord and master was Prince Vladimir, later to become the Great Prince of Kiev. It was Vladimir who established the Greek Orthodox faith in Russia, converting the people of Kiev in a mass baptism in 988. The bold-spirited Novgorodians, however, were loath to part with their old gods, particularly with Peroun, the god of thunder and lightning and patron of warriors, whose immense statue with a silver head and golden moustache stood on the bank of Lake Ilmen, with eight sacrificial bonfires burning around it day and night. Up until the twentieth century, travellers sailing past this site, called Peryn, would throw a coin into the water to avert possible misfortune. Faced by the people's stubbornness, Prince Vladimir sent warriors to Novgorod to convert the populace to Christianity and it was only after several bloody skirmishes that the townspeople were driven into the river to be baptized. The army remained in the city afterwards, while the now ostensibly Christian Novgorodians completed the construction of a thirteen-domed wooden church.

Wood was the main material used for building as well as for many domestic objects, since all the territory around Novgorod was covered in thick forests. Because wood does not rot in the marshy Novgorodian soil, archaeologists have been able to uncover much of the city's past. Their meticulous street-by-street excavations have revealed layers of ancient pavements consisting of split wooden logs, in the crevices of which have been found many objects of the past, including rings, hair-combs, chess pieces, coins and many letters written on scrolls of thin birch-bark. The same layout of buildings has been found in different quarters of the city: a big house belonging to the master – a merchant

or boyar – in the centre of the plot, with outhouses, servants' quarters, larders and stables, surrounded by craftsmen's workshops; some places boasted a church of their own. The layout reflects a clan settlement where every man could turn soldier at a moment's notice and where the united strength of several clans banded together could make or break the city's rulership.

By the early eleventh century Vladimir had been succeeded by his son Yaroslav as Prince of Novgorod and in 1014 Yaroslav defied his father by refusing to pay the traditional yearly tribute to Kiev. The angry Vladimir died before he was able to set out with his army against his recalcitrant son and no tribute was ever subsequently paid by Novgorod. Moreover, when Yaroslav became Prince of Kiev (1019–54), he granted more liberties to Novgorod.

The money usually payable to Kiev may have been used towards building a mighty stone wall around the Detinets in 1044 and, in the centre of this fortress, Novgorod's first stone church. Seeking to emphasize his own and the city's independence, the Prince dedicated the church to St Sophia and gave orders for a building comparable in size and shape to St Sophia in Kiev. It had five naves, with an open gallery running along three of its sides, but, unlike St Sophia in Kiev with its thirteen domes, the church in Novgorod had only six, five central ones and the sixth crowning a square tower adjoining the church's south-western corner. The tower's staircase led up to a broad gallery for the use of the Prince and his retinue. Novgorod did not need the many galleries with auxiliary rooms of Kiev's St Sophia – the main church of all Russia and the temporal as well as spiritual centre of the great Kievian principality – and hence it did not have the many domes that topped the drums built to house such galleries and rooms. Novgorod's St Sophia also looked much more austere than its counterpart in Kiev since the Novgorodians had no coloured marble or sparkling tiles for decorating it.

THE CENTRE OF THE DETINETS (*left and above*).

There is, however, a special quality to the stone buildings in Novgorod that is not found elsewhere. Whereas in Kiev and other southern cities, the buildings were made from big, flat bricks called plynth, Novgorodians had a local building tradition based on Western techniques. Walls were made of granite boulders, slate and brick, plastered over with mortar which was smoothed down but never polished. The slightly uneven, massive surfaces give the impression that a giant has moulded them and produce a play of sunlight, shadow and half-tones that imparts a romantic flavour to the local architecture.

The majestic Church of St Sophia was begun in 1045 and completed in 1050, the same year as the cathedral in Trier, one of the most famous cathedrals in Germany built in the Romanesque style; St Mark in Venice would not be started for another thirteen years; and the austere temples in Spain's Santiago de Compostela and Winchester Cathedral in England not for another fifteen and nineteen years respectively. St Sophia soon became the symbol of Novgorod, its city temple; Novgorodians would set out to war with the cry 'Let us stand for St Sophia' and they would leave their fortunes and their most prized war trophies to the church when they died.

The door of the western portico was brought in 1187 from the Swedish capital, Sigtuna, which had been captured by the Novgorodians. Its halves are made up of bronze plates with bas-reliefs, mostly scenes from the New and Old Testaments, with an inscription in Latin above each. It is probable that the Swedes themselves had seized the door as a war trophy, for it carries a sculpted portrait of Bishop Wiechmann of Magdeburg (1152–92). At that time Magdeburg was famous for the craftsmanship of its smelters and casters, and the lower left half of the door shows two casters with their scales and pincers; their names, Rikwin and Weissmut, are inscribed above. When the door first arrived in Russia, it probably needed repairs. At this time the Russian translations would have been supplied for the Latin inscriptions and a third figure holding a hammer and tongs inserted between the original two. Above this portrayal of a proud medieval Novgorodian craftsman is the Russian inscription, 'Master Avraam'.

Contacts with Europeans and extensive trade with them promoted the flourishing of literacy and crafts, and Novgorod became known for its copiers of books, its artists, builders and armourers. It is not therefore surprising that the oldest surviving Russian book, dating from 1065, comes from Novgorod: a Gospel manuscript of 292 white parchment sheets with beautiful illuminations and vignettes, commissioned by Ostromir, the city mayor, who was a

THE CATHEDRAL OF ST SOPHIA AND THE BELL TOWER SEEN BEHIND THE WALLS OF THE DETINETS FROM ACROSS THE VOLKHOV RIVER.

close friend and possibly a relation of the princely family. It was found by accident in one of the Moscow Kremlin churches in 1720 and Tsar Peter the Great ordered it to be brought to St Petersburg, where it was again lost and only discovered anew in 1805, nine years after the death of Catherine II, among the Empress's old dresses. Since then, the Gospel has been carefully preserved in the Leningrad Public Library.

Almost as soon as St Sophia was completed, and under the Church's auspices, one of the first Russian historical chronicles was started. Including several caustic remarks about the Prince of Kiev, the chronicle exudes Novgorod's spirit of freedom and independence, and asserts a special role for the city in the history of the Russian lands. Such free-thinking could only have been possible if sanctioned by powerful and influential persons, who were probably the Archbishop of Novgorod, whose residence stood by St Sophia within the Detinets walls, and clan leaders from different ends of the city.

A characteristic feature of Novgorod was the powerful merchants' and craftsmen's guilds, which followed the West European model. The first and most important among them was the corporation of merchants trading in beeswax, whose spiritual and political centre was the large church of Ivan-on-the-Opokas, built in 1127. Here sat the merchants' court, arbitrating in all kinds of commercial conflicts, and here too were kept the city's standards of weights and measures. Not far from this church was that of St Paraskeva Piatnitsa, which served as a kind of club for the merchants controlling all Novgorodian trade with the West. First built of wood in 1156, the church was rebuilt in stone in 1206 by the corporation.

Both of these churches have come down to our time in good repair. They stand on the Commercial side, that is the right bank of the Volkhov, which was mainly populated by Russian and foreign merchants. The left bank, where the Detinets stands, was known as the Sophiiskaya side, after St Sophia. There was intense rivalry, at first secret and then open, between the sides, but gradually the merchants, who owned the better part of the city's wealth, gained an advantage over their competitors.

Reflecting this rivalry, in 1116 Prince Mstislav of Novgorod attempted to demonstrate his power and concern for the city by building new fortified walls around the Detinets, adding considerably to the fortress's area. But the merchants and aristocracy of Novgorod had determined to seize power and twenty years later, in 1136, there was a rising against the Prince, actively encouraged by the upper classes. The princely authority was rejected and the Prince

THE CHURCH OF ST PARASKEVA PIATNITSA IN THE COMMERCIAL SIDE (*top and above*).

himself exiled. The Novgorodians, now free to decide on their own form of government and defence, had *condottieri* stationed outside the city walls and set up a ruling council, the *veche*, consisting of representatives of the local artistocracy, guild elders and the archbishop. When necessary, the council had a right, by sounding the *veche* bell, to call a general meeting of the burghers to discuss matters of urgency. On such occasions, emotions frequently ran high, fuelled by the rivalry between the Commercial and Sophiiskaya sides, and it was not unknown for participants to be thrown over the bridge into the waters of the Volkhov.

The principles and destiny of Novgorod's political life echo surprisingly closely those of medieval Florence, which in 1115 became an independent commune and from 1138 was ruled by consuls elected by the city council. As in Novgorod, the Florentine council had a right to call general meetings of its burghers.

Like Florence, the first Russian republic flourished and accumulated wealth for three and a half centuries. At times the Volkhov was so crowded with merchant ships that a fire which started on one bank of the river could cross from ship to ship to the other bank. Teams of Novgorodian explorers crossed the Urals and set up trading stations in Siberia, while in the city itself the best artists and craftsmen of the day adorned the churches with frescos and produced works of art that are today the pride of many a museum collection. The fame of Novgorod the Great, as it came to be known, of its victories and prosperity, lived on through the succeeding centuries and, although many disorders and difficulties lay beneath the romantic image, the Novgorod

CHURCHES IN THE COUNTRYSIDE AROUND NOVGOROD: THE 12TH-CENTURY CATHEDRAL OF ST GEORGE (*above*).

THE 14TH-CENTURY CHURCH OF OUR SAVIOUR OF THE TRANSFIGURATION-IN-ELIJAH-STREET (*top right*).

THE 12TH-CENTURY CHURCH OF THE ANNUNICATION-AT-ARKAZHI (*above*).

republic seemed an example to emulate when, in the nine-teenth century, the best minds of Russia fell to thinking about the future development of their country.

Fortune seemed indeed to favour Novgorod. In 1237, when the Tartar hordes of Khan Batu swept through Russia with sword and fire, destroying and burning its cities, Novgorod alone was left intact. The Tartars did not have the strength left to make their way through the marshes and thick forests around the city and Novgorod was given a chance to prepare for an expected invasion from the west by the Teutonic knights. Hoping for rich spoils and on a crusade to convert the Slavs to the true, that is Catholic, faith, the Teutonic knights set out against Russia in 1240, aware that the Russian lands had not recovered from the Tartar invasion. After seizing the fortress of Izborsk and, taking advantage of treachery, capturing Pskov, 'Novgorod's younger brother', they gathered all their resources

in March 1242 for a thrust against Novgorod. On 5 April they clashed with the Russian army commanded by Prince Alexander Nevsky and after a fierce battle the heavily armoured knights were finally put to rout. But the victory cost Novgorod dear. In the half century after 1240, only three churches were built in Novgorod, and those were of wood, compared to the dozens of stone buildings erected in the preceding century, and it was not until the end of the thirteenth century that Novgorod managed to reach its former level of life and trade.

Because Novgorod had never been captured by enemies, it became a unique example of medieval Russian architecture. Over forty churches dating from the twelfth to the seventeenth century have been preserved within the residential areas of the Commercial and Sophiiskaya sides, besides the Detinets itself. In the early fourteenth century, the Novgorodians decided to raise new stone walls round

STONE WALLS AROUND THE DETINETS BUILT IN THE 14TH AND 15TH CENTURIES.

the Detinets, replacing those built in 1116 by the Prince. The work was not concluded until the beginning of the fifteenth century and by the end of the century the walls and towers had again to be rebuilt in order to withstand cannon fire. These walls, 1385 metres (1515 yards) long, have survived to our time, along with nine of the thirteen towers. A tremendous fire in 1745 destroyed the others, including the tallest and most beautiful, the Prechistenskaya (Most Holy) tower, guarding the main gates on the Volkhov side, which was replaced by the arch still to be seen today.

It is the Kukui watch-tower that now soars proudly over the Detinets. The work of master builder Yefimov, it was erected next to the house of the *voivode*, or governor-general of Novgorod, in the late seventeenth century. At 34 metres (112 feet) high, it was used by soldiers specially detailed to watch for the approach of possible enemies, which probably accounts for its name of Kukui, from the Dutch *koke*, 'look well'.

For height and balanced proportions, Kukui had a worthy rival in the Chasozvonnaya (Tower of the Chiming Clock), which was built in the 1670s in the residence of the Metropolitan of Novgorod. (The head of the church in Novgorod had the rank of archbishop until 1590, when the first Russian patriarch was elected, and the Archbishop of Novgorod was promoted to the rank of metropolitan.) Given the dates of the two towers, it is very likely that Kukui was built as the governor-general's reply to the metropolitan's move in their long struggle for supreme authority over the city. Their residences were, provocatively, quite close, that of the governor-general in the south-west corner of the Detinets and the metropolitan's in the north-west.

Few could think of competing with the head of the church, who from the mid-twelfth century was elected from only the noblest and richest families of Novgorod and on election had to pay a large sum in gold into the city treasury. It was therefore only a handful of particularly wealthy burghers who might hope to outrival the magnificence of the metropolitan's house. One merchant, Sotko Sytinych, did however become famed for his treasures and his rich manor house. He is mentioned several times by the chroniclers and became the hero of several sagas.

Another Novgorodian who became well known was Archbishop Yephimy, an ardent supporter of the city's independence and a lover of architecture. At the end of the 1420s he invited a company of master masons from Germany to build him a new palace complex. Its heart was the Chamber of Facets building, on the top floor of which was a spacious hall with Gothic vaulting supported by a single, central pillar. Some thirty years after it was built, this hall

was taken as the model for the refectory in the Troitsa-Sergieva (Trinity and St Sergius) Monastery at Zagorsk and, in turn, the refectory was imitated in the construction of the Chamber of Facets in the Moscow Kremlin. The archbishop's place included various other buildings – the ecclesiastical court of justice, the archbishop's office, a school, barns and stables – and also a watch-tower. Although this collapsed two centuries later, it was replaced by another, the 'Tower of the Chiming Clock'. The beautiful palace buildings still survive but in very poor condition.

It was also due to Archbishop Yephimy that a new bell tower was built west of St Sophia in 1439. It followed the local tradition, being built as part of a strong wall with the bells suspended in the arches. This unusual type of bell tower has survived only in Novgorod, Pskov and other north-western border towns, its imposing nature reflecting Novgorod's position as a powerful stronghold.

THE BELL TOWER OF ST SOPHIA – THE BELLS WHICH USED TO HANG IN THE ARCHES NOW STAND IN FRONT.

The Novgorodian archbishops did not, however, enjoy their power for long. Despite, or because of, its great wealth, the city was unable to retain its independence between the two powerful states of Muscovy and Lithuania, one of which had clearly to be chosen as overlord. The nobles preferred the Lithuanian duke, hoping to extract more privileges from him, but the ordinary citizens preferred Muscovy, with which they shared a common language and faith. The Muscovy ruler, Ivan III, taking advantage of the discord and relying on support from the people, arrived in Novgorod in early 1478 with a small army. He was welcomed by the townspeople and the next day set up a court to hear their complaints. The reprisals were comparatively mild: 150 people were executed and fifteen thousand noble families resettled in central Russia. Ivan III levied a duty on the city and all the monasteries, and, according to the Polish chronicler Dlugosz, he carried out of Novgorod, in February 1478, 300 cartloads of gold, silver and precious stones. The city bell which had convened the burghers to council meetings was also taken to Moscow under guard, as if under arrest. Novgorod thus lost its herald of freedom.

The freedom-loving Novgorodian republic had also given birth to various Christian heresies. In the late fourteenth and early fifteenth centuries, it had been the source of the spreading 'Strigolnik' heresy, and at the end of the fifteenth century of the 'Judaite' heresy, which soon spread as far as Moscow and found many supporters in Tsar Ivan III's court. Even the Tsar himself was influenced, which may have affected his treatment of the Novgorodians.

His grandson Tsar Ivan the Terrible was, however, set on stamping out all remnants of Novgorod's past freedoms. Using the excuse of a forged and planted letter that revealed a treacherous switch of allegiance by Novgorod to the Lithuanian sovereign, he sent an army from Moscow in 1570 to surround the city. The burghers gave themselves up to the mercy of the tyrant, and trials and executions promptly followed. Between 500 and 1000 people were sentenced to death every day and historians have estimated that at least 60,000 people lost their lives, with the toll made more grim by lack of food and by epidemics. A census taken in 1627 put the population of Novgorod at 1000, and the city never recovered. Even 250 years later, the population was only slightly over 20,000.

By the middle of the nineteenth century Novgorod was an ordinary provincial town, but its famous past was suddenly recognized when Tsar Alexander II decided to celebrate the millennium of Russia in 1862 by erecting a monument there. The decision was influenced by the Tsar's serious concern, following his abolition of serfdom the previous year, about the growing nihilism in Russia, which he hoped to counteract by pointing to the greatness of the country's past under its sovereigns. If the idea had been thought of earlier, Kiev, as the older city, might have been chosen for a millennium celebration a decade before. However, Kiev symbolized the Ukraine, whereas Novgorod stood for Russia, and it was the biggest of the surviving old Russian towns. Moreover, its founding date of 862 coincided with several anniversaries and the unveiling ceremony was deliberately set for 28 August, 1862 to take

THE MONUMENT BUILT TO CELEBRATE THE MILLENNIUM OF RUSSIA IN 1862.

advantage of these. On that day seven years before, Alexander II had been crowned in Moscow and fifty years before, Russian troops had withstood Napoleon in the Battle of Borodino. It was also the date that, four centuries earlier, had marked the start of the rule of Duke Ivan III, who was the first to assume the title of sovereign, or tsar, and it was the centenary of the ascent to the throne of Empress Catherine II (1762–96).

The ceremony took place in the square in front of St Sophia in the middle of the Detinets, where the enormous monument was unveiled. Based on the design of the Monomach crown, the ancient crown of the Grand Dukes of Russia, it consists of a round pedestal surmounted by a globe representing the orb of state, topped by a cross and surrounded by life-sized figures of outstanding people from Russian political history, the sciences, literature and the arts from the tenth to the mid-nineteenth century. In contrast with the severe beauty of ancient St Sophia, the huge monument looks restless and overcrowded with figures.

The millennium monument was dismantled by the Germans during their occupation of Novgorod in the Second World War. They intended to take it to Germany, but before they could do so the city was freed, on 20 January 1944, by Russian troops. Novgorod had been badly damaged, many of its houses destroyed, and in the centre of the Detinets the frozen limbs of dead soldiers and the bronze figures from the monument were sticking out of the thick shroud of snow. The monument has subsequently been restored, along with many other historical buildings. Specialists are continuing to try to piece together fragments of medieval frescos and archaeological excavations are constantly yielding new finds to add to the collection in the local history museum. An unusual new museum has been opened on the outskirts of Novgorod that shows examples of traditional Russian wooden architecture, and is a further tribute to the historic city of Novgorod.

TRADITIONAL BUILDINGS IN THE MUSEUM OF WOODEN ARCHITECTURE.

PSKOV

This north-western city lies on a high promontory at the confluence of the Pskova and Velikaya rivers, close to Lake Peipus and the Baltic Sea, and its long role in defending Russia's western borders shows in the formidable strength of its surviving fortifications and thick-walled houses and churches. Settlers appeared here in the fifth to sixth centuries and the earliest fortress had been established some time before Pskov's first mention in the chronicles in 903, when Igor, the future Prince of Kiev, married a local woman called Olga. She was converted to Christianity in Constantinople in 955 and it was her grandson, the great Prince Vladimir of Kiev, who at the end of the century would make Christianity the official religion of the Kievan principality and its outlying territories, including Pskov.

Arrogant, far-off Kiev had, however, less influence on Pskov than its rich neighbour and Kiev's trading rival, Novgorod, for which Pskov provided protection from potential enemy attacks in return for trade openings and financial and military support. Often called 'Novgorod's younger brother', Pskov later followed the lead of its big brother in its republican method of government, at first overseen by a governor-general from Novgorod, and in its guilds. Yet there were differences in outlook, shown perhaps most clearly in the Novgorod and Pskov schools of icon painting. The former emulated the Byzantine tradition, with a central full- or half-length image of a saint balanced by scenes from the saint's life painted in the borders; bright red and white was the favourite colour combination. Pskov icons, in contrast, were generally asymmetrical, top heavy, in composition but were more expressive and used intense, sometimes sombre colours – often darkish greens against yellow or golden backgrounds.

The ruling council, as in Novgorod, could convene Pskov's burghers when necessary and they would gather in the square outside the Trinity Cathedral, the principal church of the Pskov region, which housed the city's documents and where the councillors met. Rebuilt in the seventeenth century, the huge, white-walled cathedral supported by powerful buttresses stands at the highest point of the promontory and on a clear day its silver domes can be seen against the skies from far away.

The princes invited to govern and defend Pskov lived next to the cathedral in a powerful fortress, its original wooden walls being replaced in the mid-thirteenth century by walls of thick stone slabs. Restored, they are still impressively threatening today, although over the centuries they have lost at least a third of their original height. At the urging of Prince Dovmont, the bustling market town that grew up around the fortress was also encircled by stone walls in the mid-thirteenth century and when 'Dovmont's Town' expanded, another wall was built in the early fourteenth century, creating the so-called 'Middle Town'. Pskov continued to grow, achieving full independence in 1348, and a further line of fortifications was built in the late fourteenth century to encompass the ever increasing city. The Middle Town wall was demolished in the fifteenth century and a fifth wall was built to defend the burghers who had now moved to the opposite river banks. The city's walls were reinforced and heightened in the 1570s, and have survived to the present.

Many of Pskov's old buildings have been preserved, among them the city's oldest monastery, St Saviour, built in 1156 by Byzantine masters. Its white-plastered walls are surmounted by a single dome and, although the building and the original frescos have been heavily restored, the church stands as a monument to provincial Byzantine art. Also still surviving is the twelfth-century church of the Ivanovsky nunnery, burial place of the first Pskov duchesses, and the Snetogorsky Monastery, on the outskirts of the city, whose church is painted with beautiful fourteenth-century frescos.

What gives Pskov's medieval architecture its remarkable character is its defensive border role. Such churches as St

Basil's-on-the-Hill, St Paul and St Peter, and Archangel Michael are distinctive in their austere, almost square outlines, their thick, plain walls built to withstand attack; outbuildings and galleries are rare additions. Equally distinctive are the belfries, originally, as in St Nicholas-on-the-Dry, erected on the church roof, with bells suspended from the keystones within several small arches, but from the late fifteenth century built as a separate, fortified tower on a high, solid foundation which provided a safe storage place; an example is that of the Church of the Dormition-at-the-Ferry.

A seventeenth-century plan of Pskov shows 39 fortified towers, each with a small church as the defenders' last refuge. A sixteenth-century example of the latter, by a corner of the fortress wall, has recently been restored, and in fact consists of two churches nestling against each other which, for economy, were built with a common wall. In houses, too, defence was the first necessity and the affluent merchants' surviving residences are similarly severe and powerful in appearance, each a small fortress; thick expanses of stone walls, the windows protected by iron shutters, solid, broad columns able to support the weight of heavy floors and ceilings, and double iron doors. Within, on the first or second storey, were large drawing- and dining-rooms decorated with murals and chintzes and reached by broad ornamental staircases.

The pragmatism of Pskov's burghers helped it to escape the fate of Novgorod, destroyed by Ivan the Terrible, for in 1510, when faced with the danger of losing the city's independence to their strong Polish neighbour, they had willingly accepted the rule of the Grand Prince of Moscow, Vasili III. Pskov continued to prosper, and in its thousand-year history it has withstood numerous sieges and attacks, and survived the German occupation and destruction of World War II – a past that lives on in its powerful old city walls and many historic buildings.

IZBORSK

Thirty kilometres (19 miles) south-west of Pskov rises a large hill on which the powerful fortress of Izborsk was established by the Norse prince, Truvor, before the ninth century. Its moat and the remnants of its once mighty earth ramparts can still be seen; and by the former entrance to the stronghold stands the austere seventeenth-century Church of St Nicholas, built on the site of the original wooden church. In the fourteenth century, this wooden fortress was abandoned and a new fortress built on nearby

Zhuravlinaya (Crane) Hill, a massive stone structure, triangular in shape, with tall, colossally powerful towers and stone crosses along the top of the high wall. Next to the main gates of this surviving citadel is a church, built close to the wall and capable of being used as another fortified tower if necessary. The neighbouring tall bell tower acted as a look-out post; it was repaired in the late nineteenth century, when a skeleton was found in the foundations.

PSKOVO-PECHERSKY MONASTERY

Like Izborsk, this monastery was part of the chain of powerful border fortifications designed to protect the rich cities of Novgorod and Pskov. Lying to the north-west of Izborsk, about 50 kilometres (30 miles) from Pskov, it began in the fifteenth century as a small community of Christians living in caves in the sandstone cliff rising above a stream. In 1473 they founded a church in one of the crevices, naming it after the Church of the Dormition in Kiev's Pechersky Monastery; apart from the eighteenth-century façade, it remains unaltered. Half a century later, the monks emphasized their spiritual links with Russia's first monastery when they dedicated a church to St Anthony and St Theodosius, founders of the Kiev Monastery.

In 1553 the father superior, Kornily, decided to build a powerful wall to protect the monastery against possible attack from the Livonian knights who had built a fortress, Neuhausen, just across the border. The ever suspicious Ivan the Terrible, believing that the monastery was about to break away from Russia, came here and personally murdered Kornily; the path from the gate to the main church along which the father's body was carried has since been known as the Bloody Way. The walls built by Kornily withstood assaults by Polish and Swedish armies on six occasions between 1581 and 1703, and are still standing.

One of the monastery's treasures is a sixteenth-century painted wood-carving of St Nicholas, a rare example of the art of sculpting figures in low relief from a thick wooden base, then painting them: a technique developed to avoid the Russian Orthodox Church's ban on 'heathen' three-dimensional images, which lasted till the eighteenth century. The monastery's present art workshop was established after World War II but otherwise time has changed little. From the entranceway by the Church of the Dormition, six pathways stretch more than 200 metres (650 feet) into the hillside, the tombs of past generations of monks buried in the walls of the galleries, and in the farthest cells live the monks who have taken the vow of silence.

THE STATE OF MOSCOW

VLADIMIR
BOGOLYUBOVO AND SUZDAL

The vast tracts of land east and north-east of Moscow had become an outlying part of the powerful Kievan principality by the tenth century, conquered by the trading adventurers who came to obtain furs from the hunters and trappers here. Those fleeing oppression in Kiev and Novgorod frequently found refuge in this remote region of forests, rivers and lakes, where the harsh natural conditions helped determine the resolute character of its people. A rebellion against Kiev in 1024 (36 years after the introduction of Christianity to Russia) was crushed and the area continued as a possession of the principality. It was Prince Vladimir Monomach, married to an English princess, who in 1108 founded a small fortress on the high ridge at the confluence of the Rivers Lybed and Klyazma, naming it after himself. When he became Prince of Kiev in 1113, the north-eastern Russian lands came under the lordship of first his younger son Yuri Dolgoruki, the founder of Moscow, and then, after 1155, Yuri Dolgoruki's son Andrei.

After many years of acting as his ambitious father's political adviser, Prince Andrei determined to establish himself as a rival ruler in his own far-off lands. He fled Kiev overnight with his family and trusted guards, taking with him an icon of the Virgin, supposedly painted by St Luke himself. The icon, subsequently known as the Vladimir Mother of God, was held in such veneration that its possession would enable Andrei to create a cult on which to build his powerful state. (The often-restored icon, painted by an early twelfth-century Byzantine artist, is now kept in the Tretyakov Gallery in Moscow.)

Knowing that he could draw on the support of its merchants and artisans against the opposition of the boyars, Andrei chose Vladimir as his capital. The town founded by his grandfather was expanded and a whole new town built to the east, both surrounded by a wall seven kilometres (four and a half miles) long – longer than that around Kiev. The main entrance in the west was rebuilt on the model of Kiev and, like it, named the Golden Gates. However, the most important new construction was the Cathedral of the Dormition, built between 1158 and 1160 by master masons brought to Vladimir from Western Europe, all of them from the court of the German emperor, Frederick Barbarossa. The stately cathedral with its white stone walls and gilded columns included exotic carvings of strutting peacocks and animal masks besides many biblical figures, and its interior was painted by Greek artists and furnished with precious fabrics and gold and silver ornaments.

Prince Andrei did not, however, live to see all his ambitious dreams fulfilled. In June 1174 he was murdered by a group of boyars, fearful of the expansion of his powers and the increasing influence of the merchants in the city. After two years of violence and popular rebellion, Andrei's younger brother, Prince Vsevolod – nicknamed the Big Nest because of his numerous children – took over the throne and continued the expansion of Vladimir. A new line of defences was built around the city, to include its eastern part, and European architects were employed to erect a stone wall around his palace and the cathedral.

THE CATHEDRAL OF THE DORMITION: THE WEST FRONT (*right*), LACY BRONZE DECORATION ON THE WEST PORTICO (*above*), AND THE GOLDEN DOMES (*overleaf*).

In 1194–97, the beautifully proportioned Cathedral of St Demetrius of Salonica, patron saint of the Slavs, was built. In Romanesque style, the walls were designed in three tiers: the lower, and tallest, bare of decoration; the middle consisting of a narrow band of blind arcading with carved half columns framing the carved images of saints and resting on corbels in the form of lions, birds or griffins; and the high, third tier pierced by narrow windows in splendidly carved frames. The reliefs in the *zakomaras* – the semi-circular upper sections of the walls – included portrayals of King Solomon, Alexander the Great and Prince Vsevolod himself, seated on the throne. Unfortunately, the cathedral was much altered as the result of a visit to the city in 1837 by Tsar Nikolai I, who ordered the removal of the old galleries surrounding the cathedral and the two towers before the western façade which had linked the cathedral with the wings of the royal palace.

The reign of Vsevolod marked the heyday of Vladimir-on-Klyazma, but sadly few of the buildings have survived from that time. After a terrible fire in 1185, which destroyed eighty-two of the city's churches, the Cathedral of the Dormition was repaired and new walls built around it, concealing the former splendour of the multicoloured décor. The cathedral became bigger and more solemn; not as light and exultant as before. Today, remnants of the original western wall can be seen in the narthex and the interior includes fragments of twelfth-century paintings.

The Tartar invasion by Khan Batu caused wholesale destruction of Vladimir in 1238 and the city which had been trying to exceed the glory of Kiev met the same tragic fate as its parent. The royal palace was destroyed, along with the palace of the Bishop of Vladimir; the city's walls and the fortress protecting the cathedrals of the Dormition and St Demetrius were razed.

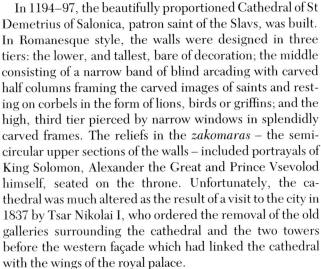

THE CATHEDRAL OF ST DEMETRIUS OF SALONICA (*above*).
STONE IMAGES ON THE THIRD TIER OF THE FAÇADE (*left*).

THE NORTH DOOR OF THE CATHEDRAL (*above*).

One building that has survived is the Princess's Convent, founded by the wife of Prince Vsevolod in the early twelfth century. The fifteenth-century church inside the covent is a precise imitation of the original, using ordinary bricks, whitewashed in keeping with tradition, instead of the original 'plinthos' or big, flat bricks. Here the Princess was buried, as were the wife and daughter of Prince Alexander Nevsky. The military hero himself was buried in the Monastery of the Nativity, close to St Demetrius, of which only part of the eighteenth-century wall now survives. Alexander Nevsky's remains were transferred from Vladimir to the newly built St Petersburg in the early eighteenth century; they disappeared in the 1917 Revolution but the splendid silver coffin that held them is now on display in the Hermitage.

Vladimir never fully recovered from the Tartar invasion, although it enjoyed a brief revival in the early fourteenth century after Metropolitan Maksim moved from ravaged Kiev in 1299 to Vladimir, which became Russia's new spiritual centre until 1326, when Metropolitan Pyotr transferred to Moscow. In recognition of this move, Vasili Yermolin was sent from Moscow later in the fourteenth century to restore several ruined churches and the city's Golden Gates. The celebrated painter Andrei Rublev also visited Vladimir and redecorated the Cathedral of the Dormition, where some of his striking, elegant frescos can still be seen today.

Over the following centuries, Vladimir remained a small provincial town and in the nineteenth century became a place of exile for dissenters, including the writer Alexander Herzen who, in 1847, moved to London where he established the first major independent Russian printing press. The town was on the route to Siberia and convicts in irons were marched through its main street, a scene portrayed by Isaak Levitan (1860–1900) in his painting *Vladimirka*. Today, Vladimir is an industrial centre, with new residential neighbourhoods and impersonal concrete buildings masking the glories of its past.

BOGOLYUBOVO

From Vladimir, originally through the now long-gone Silver Gates, the road leads east to the village of Bogolyubovo, past a prehistoric settlement where archaeologists have discovered two burial chambers containing skeletons, dating from 23,000 years ago, and many remarkable artefacts, including daggers and spears carved from mammoth tusks, and thousands of bone beads; the finds are now in the local museum. The village is set high on the hillside, giving

fine views of the landscape, but there is little trace of the original church and palace which Prince Andrei built here in the mid-twelfth century.

According to legend, the horses bearing the precious icon of the Virgin which Andrei had brought with him from Kiev halted ten kilometres (six miles) before reaching Vladimir and could not be induced to proceed. Taking this as a sign from God, Andrei named the place Bogolyubovo ('loved by God'), a name he also took for himself, and decided to build a church and a royal residence there. Situated at the confluence of the Rivers Nerl and Klyazma, waterways running the length of north-eastern Russia, the site was a strategic point for controlling all local trade.

All that now remains of Prince Andrei's palace is the staircase tower – on the spiral steps of which Andrei was supposedly murdered – and the passage that connected with the royal church. After his violent death, the palace was plundered by Prince Gleb of Ryazan and subsequently destroyed by the Tartars. At the very end of the thirteenth

century a small monastery was built on the ruins, which achieved prominence after the Prince was made a saint by the Russian Church, at which time the original wall was replaced by that which exists today. A huge bell tower over the gate was added in the nineteenth century and a massive church built in neo-Byzantine style, using many of the white-stone slabs from the original structure.

The royal church that was at the heart of the palace complex survived till the seventeenth century, when alterations to enlarge the monastery caused the ancient building to collapse; part of the northern wall, adjoining the passageway to the palace, almost miraculously remained. Some idea of the church's lightness and grace can be gained from the nearby Church of the Intercession on the Nerl, built at the same time by the same architects. This small, single-domed church looks as though it has been hewn out of a single piece of stone of unusual whiteness; everything about it is beautifully proportioned. It is similar to Vladimir's St Demetrius but much more delicate.

SUZDAL

Further along the road from Bogolyubovo, rising from one of the hills in the undulating countryside, is the remarkable town of Suzdal, famed for its school of icon painting and for many forms of applied art, as well as a place of imprisonment for the tsars' disgraced courtiers. The town seen today, with its numerous bell towers rising like fir trees against the horizon, took shape in the eighteenth century but Suzdal was a centre of lively trade as far back as the twelfth century and its unique charm lies in the fact that it never abandoned the architectural traditions of the twelfth to sixteenth centuries

Among its many beautiful buildings is the Cathedral of the Nativity, originally built in the early twelfth century by Prince Vladimir, the founder of the city of Vladimir. It was rebuilt by Prince Yuri Dolgoruki and later by his grandson; this third building of white stone survived till the fifteenth century when its upper part collapsed. The five heavy

WOODEN PEASANT HOUSES IN VILLAGES BETWEEN VLADIMIR AND SUZDAL (*above and left*); PAINTED AND DECORATED WITH INTRICATE CARVING.

THE MUSEUM OF WOODEN ARCHITECTURE AND PEASANT LIFE AT
SUZDAL: THE CHURCH OF THE RESURRECTION (1776) FROM THE
VILLAGE OF PATAKINO.

THE CHURCH OF THE
TRANSFIGURATION FROM
KOZLYATYEVO (1756).

domes seen today were added to the old base when the cathedral was rebuilt in 1528. It is decorated with fine carvings, many of lions, the heraldic beast of the Vladimir princedom, but its most glorious craftsmanship is shown in the so-called Golden Gates of the southern and western portals, made by local craftsmen in the thirteenth century. The series of copper plates etched in gold depict stories of the Virgin and the Archangel Michael, the glittering reliefs framed by carved white-stone portals. Within is the splendid iconostasis of gilded copper made in the seventeenth century by the court artist Grigori Zinoviev.

The cathedral was built within the walls of the Suzdal Kremlin, of which traces remain of the rampart and moat.

To the north stood the prince's palace, which included the royal Church of the Dormition; the present stone church was built in 1650, replacing the original wooden structure. Nearby are the Archbishop's Chambers, a variety of structures dating from the sixteenth and seventeenth centuries, built on the former Bishop's Chambers, and now housing various museums with many examples of the fine icons and artistry for which Suzdal is famed. There is also a collection of reconstructed wooden churches brought from different places in the Museum of Wooden Architecture.

By the end of the twelfth century the painters, goldsmiths, potters and other craftsmen of Suzdal formed a large community north-east of the Kremlin, protected by

THE CARVED WINDOWS AND SHUTTERS OF A TYPICAL
19TH-CENTURY PEASANT HOUSE FROM CENTRAL RUSSIA.

ramparts and a wooden wall, and with a central market place. A trading arcade was built in classical style in the early nineteenth century along its western edge. Today the area is still the city's main shopping centre and the venue of the week-long festival of *Maslenitsa*, a celebration of spring dating to pagan times when pancakes are eaten.

Although Suzdal, like the rest of Russia, was sacked by the Tartars, seven monasteries had been built around the small town by the end of the thirteenth century and by the sixteenth century there were eleven monasteries and nunneries here. The Convent of the Intercession became famous in the early sixteenth century when the Moscow Grand Prince Vasili III confined his wife here after she had born him no heir, forcing her to take the veil; he finally divorced her to marry the Polish beauty Yelena Glinskaya, mother of the future Ivan the Terrible. According to legend, however, some months after coming to the convent the first wife gave birth to a son, who was said to have died and whose tomb was shown to the agents sent from Moscow by the Prince. The child, however, supposedly survived and grew up to become the famous brigand hero Kudeyar. Excavations in 1934 did in fact reveal a tiny wooden coffin, within which was a rag-doll dressed in a pearl-embroidered shirt.

Many other high-born women were confined in the convent over the following centuries, including, in 1698, Peter the Great's first wife, who was moved to a stricter convent twenty years later after she had been implicated in a plot against the Tsar by the Tsarevich Alexei. The history of the Convent of the Intercession does not, however, detract from the charm of its architecture.

The church is very similar outwardly to that of the Convent of the Deposition of the Robe, also built in the sixteenth century. The walls and towers of the convent have a beautiful, airy look, almost like stage scenery, in contrast to the stout, fortress-like walls of the Monastery of the Saviour and St Euthimius on the high right bank of the Kamenka. Entered through a massive tower and small courtyard with the austere Gatechurch of the Annunciation, the monastery centres on the imposing Church of the Transfiguration, built in 1594. The square fronting it ends on the right in the early sixteenth-century belfry, its octagonal tower crowned by a tall and slender, pyramid-shaped roof which was among the earliest of such traditional tent roofs to be built in stone rather than wood.

Besides the monasteries and nunneries which form the architectural centres of Suzdal, there are nearly thirty churches dotted along the streets and lanes, and to walk around the city is a constant source of pleasant surprises.

THE MARKET PLACE, TORGOVAYA SQUARE, FLANKED BY THE CLASSICAL TRADING ARCADE AND THE CHURCH OF THE RESURRECTION (1720).

MOSCOW

To tell the entire story of Moscow, or even of the Kremlin alone, with its wealth of ancient buildings and unique museums, is not possible here, and this account is inevitably to some extent subjective in its coverage. The obvious starting point is, however, the Kremlin, surrounded by powerful red-brick battlements and towers, for this is the heart of the huge capital city which sprawls over an area of nearly 900 square kilometres (350 square miles) and is home to nearly nine million people.

Kremlin, *krem* or *kremnik* is Old Russian for a fortress protecting a castle or the principal part of a town, and the earliest fortifications here date to the eleventh century, although from archaeological studies it is known that people were living on the Kremlin hill as far back as 2000 B.C. Moscow is, however, commonly dated to the year A.D. 1147, when it was first mentioned in historical chronicles as the place where the Kievan prince, Yuri Dolgoruki (meaning Long Arm – from his far-reaching military exploits), invited his kinsman and military ally Prince Svyatoslav to a war council in what was then a small settlement amidst dense woods. Eight centuries later, a monument was erected to Yuri Dolgoruki, the founder of Moscow, in one of the city's main squares, facing the Municipal Council buildings.

The first Moscow Kremlin was set on a triangular promontory, roughly where the Armoury is now. A deep moat and a wall of thick oak trunks protected it on the east, while the wide River Moskva flanked it on the south and the River Neglinka on the west. The park that now stretches along the western wall was created in the early nineteenth century, when a tunnel was built to enclose the Neglinka. The archaeological story of the early fortress is shown in the museum located in the crypt of the Cathedral of the Annunciation, which stands atop the Kremlin hill.

Over the next three hundred years, the Kremlin gradually expanded and at the turn of the fifteenth century a Milanese architect, Pietro Antonio Solari, was given the task of encircling it with new battlements, which are what is seen today. The event is recorded on an inscription on the Spassky Tower, the greatest of the Kremlin's nineteen towers. The massive wall runs for 2,235 metres (7333 feet), varying in height from 5 to 19 metres (16 to 62 feet) according to the terrain, and 3.5 to 6.5 metres ($11^1/_2$ to 21 feet)

THE CATHEDRAL OF THE ANNUNCIATION.

THE KREMLIN ACROSS THE RIVER MOSKVA. BEHIND THE WALLS STAND THE CATHEDRAL OF THE ARCHANGEL MICHAEL AND THE IVAN THE GREAT BELL TOWER.

book-lined study, where H.G. Wells visited him in 1920, dubbing him the 'great Kremlin dreamer', and from their long, animated discussions subsequently wrote the book *Russia in the Dark*. The clock on the wall stands at 8.15 pm, the time on 12 December 1922 when Lenin, taken ill, left the room never to return.

A door from Lenin's apartment leads to the conference room where he headed the Council of People's Commissars (now called the USSR Council of Ministers) and where, after his death in 1924, Stalin conducted the sessions of the Communist Party's Politbureau. The room was the scene of numerous political shiftings under Stalin and Krushchev's defeat of the die-hard Stalinists in 1957. Since 1958 the Lenin room has been a museum and today Mikhail Gorbachev presides over the Soviet Cabinet and the plenary sessions of the Central Committee of the Communist Party in a neo-classical building near the Kremlin's Spassky Gates, the Presidium of the Supreme Soviet. Designed in 1934 by Rerberg, it stands on the site of a fifteenth-century convent.

Political dignitaries from both West and East are usually received in the Grand Kremlin Palace, built for Tsar Nikolai I (1825–55) and taking twelve years before completion in 1849. Princely residences had stood on this slope since the fifteenth century and Nikolai I's palace replaced that built by Rastrelli in the mid-eighteenth century, which had been badly damaged during Napoleon's occupation of it in 1812. The austere, majestic structure exceeded contemporary European palaces in size as well as splendour. The royal family's private apartments were on the ground floor, sumptuously decorated using a wide variety

thick at the base and up to 4 metres (13 feet) thick at the top, wide enough for a car to be driven along. For added protection, the battlements have 1,045 merlons.

In 1935 the gilded two-headed eagles, the old Russian national emblem, topping the Kremlin's five tallest towers were replaced by five-pointed ruby-red glass stars, with the largest star – measuring 3.5 metres (11½ feet) between its points – crowning the Spassky Tower. The five dark-red stars mark off a triangle of power in the centre of the capital, for within the buildings of this area all internal and external policy decisions have been made since March 1918, when the Soviet government moved its seat from the banks of the Neva to the banks of the Moskva.

Lenin, with his wife and younger sister, moved to a government office building erected in the late eighteenth century, the former Senate, living on the top floor in almost ascetic austerity. Adjoining Lenin's living quarters is his

THE PRESIDIUM OF THE SUPREME SOVIET AND THE SPASSKY TOWER TOPPED WITH A RED STAR.

THE STATUE OF LENIN IN THE KREMLIN GARDENS (*above*).
THE COUNCIL OF MINISTERS BUILDING (*right*).
DOMES OF THE CHURCHES OF THE TEREM PALACE (*overleaf*).

of fabrics, rare wood, bronze, china, rock crystal and tortoise-shell. The first floor, for formal occasions, has five huge halls dedicated to the orders of the Russian Empire.

The biggest and most important, the Georgian Hall, is 61 metres long by 20.5 metres wide and 17.5 metres high (200×67×57 feet), and is decorated with plaques commemorating the military Order of St George. This is where Yuri Gagarin, the first spaceman, was formally welcomed in 1961 and where foreign heads of state are usually received. Next to it is the Conference Hall, built in 1934 when the two halls of the Order of St Andrew and the Order of Alexander Nevsky were combined. Here, until 1962, the congresses of the Communist Party met.

Behind the Conference Hall in the western wing of the palace is the small but sumptuous Hall of the Order of St Catherine, often used for talks between political leaders and parliamentary delegations. The hall's predominant

colours are red, green and gold, the green reflected from malachite pilasters, together with the gilded ornate mouldings on the ceiling and doors, setting off the red of the walls, the colour associated with the Order, established by Peter I in 1714 in honour of his wife.

The Vladimir Hall in the northern wing, dedicated to the Order of Prince Vladimir, stands on what was once the Boyar Ground, the place where Russia's high nobility, the boyars, awaited audience with the monarch in the seventeenth century, and is now the venue for particularly important occasions such as the signing of foreign accords. The square hall, which appears almost circular, has rounded corners and is crowned with an octagonal dome, richly decorated with gilded stucco mouldings carved with floral patterns and symbols of the Order.

The Vladimir Hall links together the palace of Nikolai I, the palace of Tsar Alexei (1645–76) known as the Terem Palace, the Palace of Facets – built by Italian masters in the late fifteenth century and the oldest surviving civilian structure in the Kremlin – and the Palace of Congresses, erected in 1961 and the newest of all the Kremlin buildings. This huge glass and concrete rectangle replaced the Cavaliers' Quarters, the apartments for court attendants, which were used by Soviet government leaders after the 1917 Revolution until, following the Second World War, they made their homes outside Moscow.

The glass panels of the Palace of Congresses mirror the beautiful cupolas of the church of the former patriarch's palace and the gilded helmets of the biggest and most important cathedral of Moscow and Russia, the Cathedral of the Dormition. This white-stone colossus crowns the top of the Kremlin hill. It was built in the 1470s by Aristotle Fioravanti, a renowned architect from Bologna, versatile enough to be equally capable of building fortifications and casting guns. A wooden church is known to have stood on the site back in the twelfth century and the present cathedral replaced the stone church built in the late thirteenth century by the first independent Moscow prince, Daniil Alexandrovich.

To the north of the cathedral is the former residence of the head of the Russian Church, now a museum of Russian seventeenth-century life. Facing the western portal of the patriarch's residence is an ensemble of princely palaces, while to the south-east is the tall and slender Ivan the Great Bell Tower. Its name comes partly from the church on the ground floor that was dedicated to Ionas, the sixth-century father superior of a Sinai Orthodox monastery, and partly from its great height. Measuring 81 metres (266 feet) to the top of the cross, it was the tallest structure in Moscow and

A FRESCO OF THE VIRGIN AND CHILD OVER THE SOUTH DOORWAY OF THE CATHEDRAL OF THE DORMITION.

until the beginning of the twentieth century there was a decree that no building in the city should surpass the Ivan the Great Bell Tower.

The Cathedral of the Annunciation forms the southern side of Cathedral, or Tsar, Square, the main square of the Kremlin and of the whole country, where the most significant events and ceremonies in Russian history have taken place. Across this square every ruler from Daniil Alexandrovich in 1276, to the last tsar, Nikolai II, in 1896, walked to the coronation ceremony in the Cathedral of the Dormition. Funeral processions, too, crossed the square to the Cathedral of the Archangel Michael, on the southeastern corner; built in 1508, it was the burial place for all Moscow princes and tsars until Peter the Great moved his court in 1712 to St Petersburg.

The numerous gifts brought by foreign envoys for the Russian monarchs are now on display in the Armoury museum. It is a unique treasure house of precious items – sacred relics, gold and silver dishes and jewelled artefacts of all kinds. Among its collection of state regalia, which includes the thrones of Ivan the Terrible, Boris Godunov and the first tsars of the Romanov family, is the famous 'Cap of Monomach', the coronation crown of all Moscow rulers from the mid-fourteenth century to Peter the Great.

For royal banquets, gold and silver dishes were brought from the storerooms to the Palace of Facets, where feasts were held that could last for up to six hours, during which as many as 120 dishes were served. Unfortunately, the gala entrance to the palace and the staircase lined with sculptures were destroyed in the 1930s, to be replaced by a concrete box housing modern services, which has disfigured the appearance of the palace and of Cathedral Square. Inside, however, the beautiful palace remains intact; a solid, single pillar supports the vaulted roof, forming the centrepiece of the large room, which is decorated with murals depicting scenes from the Old Testament.

Sometimes, rather than give a gala dinner, the monarch might honour a foreign ambassador by sending a lavish feast to him, the numerous dishes often being carried in procession across bustling Red Square, the biggest square of medieval Moscow, then known simply as the market place. It acquired the name 'Red' (meaning beautiful in Old Russian) only after 1625, when the English architect Christopher Halloway added the shapely superstructure seen today to the previously squat Spassky Tower. Initially, the new name was associated only with the southern section of the square, where the exotic Cathedral of Basil the Blessed was built in the 1550s, on the orders of Ivan the Terrible, in commemoration of the conquest of the only

THE IVAN THE GREAT BELL TOWER (*top*). AT ITS FOOT STANDS THE MOSCOW TSAR BELL (*above*), DAMAGED DURING THE FIRE OF 1737.

RED SQUARE (*overleaf*): THE MUSEUM OF HISTORY ON THE LEFT AND THE DOMES OF THE CATHEDRAL OF ST BASIL THE BLESSED IN THE DISTANCE.

DETAILS OF THE CATHEDRAL
OF ST BASIL THE BLESSED.

remaining Tartar states in the Volga basin, the Khanates. The solemnity of the Spassky Tower now reaching up into the skies, combined with the festively coloured cathedral and the flat, white-stone platform, the Lobnoye Mesto, where government decrees were announced (and executions held), formed a beautiful ensemble.

By the end of the seventeenth century the Main Pharmacy, crowned with a colourfully decorated little tower, had been built on the northern side of the square, where the Museum of History now stands. Across the street, behind a wall decorated with brightly coloured tiles, was the Mint, which can be seen today in the courtyard of a house facing the museum. All the wooden structures were removed from the square and the whole area was cobbled, after which 'Red' came to refer to all of the square and not just the southern section.

In 1818 a monument to Prince Dmitri Pozharsky and the merchant Kuzma Minin, who had freed Moscow from Polish invaders in 1612, was erected in the centre of Red Square; the seating stadium in front of it was later replaced by the building that now houses the State Universal Store, or GUM. The ceremony to unveil the monument, the work of the sculptor Ivan Martos, marked the first of the military parades to take place in Red Square. They are now held every year on the anniversary of the 1917 Revolution.

At the beginning of the twentieth century Red Square was just another square in the city, with trams clanging across it, and it took on its present significance only after the Revolution. In 1917 those who were killed in the assault on the Kremlin and in other fighting for the Revolution were buried in common graves by the Kremlin wall. Then, in 1924, the first Lenin Mausoleum, a wooden pyramid designed by Alexei Shchusev, was erected in the centre of Red Square and was followed six years later by the tomb of marble, porphyry and granite which is seen today. The Lenin Mausoleum gave new significance to the square, which was partially rearranged to create an appearance that befitted its status. The tram tracks and overhead wires were removed, and the Minin and Pozharsky monument was shifted towards the Cathedral of St Basil the Blessed. Stands were built on either side of the Mausoleum, which acts as a podium for government leaders when the vast square is used for parades and mass rallies.

From Red Square ran the main roads to the country, to Tver and Novgorod, to Rostov and Yaroslavl, and, perhaps the oldest road in the nation, to Vladimir-on-Klyazma, for decades the capital of north-eastern Russia. In the fourteenth and fifteenth centuries, when Moscow became the centre of a powerful independent state and the River

THE STATE UNIVERSAL STORE – GUM (*top*).
RED SQUARE (*above*).

SOLDIERS GUARDING THE ENTRANCE TO THE LENIN MAUSOLEUM.
ABOVE THE DOOR, THE NAME LENIN IS SPELT OUT IN INLAID
LETTERS OF PORPHYRY.

Moskva a busy trade passage, wealthy merchants and some of the courtiers built houses on this route, which followed the river. It was known as Varvarka, after the Church of St Barbara which stood at its western end, but after 1917 the road was renamed Razin, after the leader of the peasant rebellion in the second half of the seventeenth century.

An early sixteenth-century merchant called Bobrishchev built a stone house between the Church of St Barbara and the nearby Church of Maxim the Confessor, which was appropriated by the Treasury after his death and in 1556 was presented as a gift to English merchants and diplomats by Ivan the Terrible. Thus, the first official foreign embassy building appeared in Moscow, to be followed a century later by the Holstein embassy building, also on Varvarka Street; the German traveller Adam Olearius, who published a detailed account of his journey to Muscovy, stayed there in the 1630s. At about the same time another spacious ambassadorial residence was built on a parallel street (now called Kuibyshev) north of the English Court.

Further along from the English Court on Varvarka Street is a group of sixteenth- and seventeenth-century buildings known as the Sovereign's Old Court. The boyar grandfather of Mikhail Fyodorovich, the first tsar of the Romanov dynasty, built a residence here, where Tsar Mikhail was supposedly born. The surviving structures of the Romanov estate include a three-storeyed building, of white stone with a wooden top floor, some domestic quarters and the Znamenski (or Sign) Monastery, which adjoined the estate. The boyar's residence is now a museum showing the life of the Romanov household, complete with storage cellars, formal reception room, study, children's quarters and a separate section for women.

A modern fly-over, by which guests arrive at the huge Rossia Hotel, separates the museum from the Church of St George, which dates to 1657, with the bell tower added in 1818, although the church is mentioned in chronicles in 1462. Opposite St George, on the northern side of Varvarka Street, runs Ipatievsky Lane, where there is a small town house dating to the second half of the seventeenth century, next to a modern office of the Central Committee of the Communist Party. This red and white house was the home of the court icon painter, Simon Ushakov (1626–86), who set up a school of painting here, breaking with the Byzantine tradition of icon painting and drawing on models of contemporary European portraiture.

At that time Varvarka Street was much longer, linking the Kremlin wall with the second, equally solid, wall of fortifications around Moscow known as Kitai-Gorod. Today Varvarka is a stately street, lined with important office

buildings on its northern side and with museums and exhibition halls on its southern side. Remnants of the old tower that was part of the fortifications can be seen in the underground passage leading to the Metro station.

The Kitai-Gorod wall, with its 15 towers, was built between 1535 and 1538 on the orders of Tsarina Yelena Glinskaya, mother of Ivan the Terrible. ('Kitai' means 'China' in Russian, but many scholars believe the name derives from the similar Turkish word meaning fortress.) The wall began at the Beklemish, or Moskvoretsk, Tower, which formed one of the corners of the Kremlin, and stretched eastwards along the bank of the Moskva river, abruptly turning north at the Church of St Anna in the Corner; the surviving late sixteenth-century church, with seventeenth-century chapels, is at the south-eastern corner of the Rossia Hotel, near the waterfront. From the church the wall bent north, stopping just short of the present Communist Party's Central Committee buildings, the

THE LENIN LIBRARY SITUATED ON A HILL OVERLOOKING THE KREMLIN.

THE SEVENTEENTH-CENTURY CATHEDRAL OF THE ZNAMENSKI MONASTERY ON VARVARKA STREET.

last of which was built in 1901 by Shekhtel and until 1917 was the Boyar Court Hotel. Where the wall ran west from what is now Dzerzhinsky Square, there was a wide gate that opened from Nikolskaya Street (now the Street of the October Revolution's 25th Anniversary) inside the Kremlin onto the road leading to Yaroslavl or to the tsar's hunting grounds in what is today called Sokolniki Park.

Nikolskaya Street was known as the Street of Enlightenment because of its associations with learning. The seventeenth-century church at its beginning, set in a courtyard near Red Square, is now all that remains of a monastery where a school was opened in 1665 which offered instruction in the Russian language for the first time, as well as in Greek, Latin and rhetoric. A quarter of a century later it became the Slavo-Greek-Latin Academy and among its many gifted students were the scientist Mikhail Lomonosov, the creator of Russian porcelain, Vinogradov, and the poet Kantemir, who was ambassador to England from 1732 to 1738. The neo-Gothic building halfway along Nikolskaya, which now houses the Institute of Archives and History, stands on the site of the first Russian printing shop, built in the early 1560s on the orders of Ivan the Terrible. Part of the printing shop, rebuilt in the seventeenth century, can still be seen in the courtyard of the Institute. Nearby is the site of the Hotel Slavyansky Bazaar, described by Chekhov in his novella *The Lady with the Dog* and in the restaurant of which Konstantin Stanislavsky and Vladimir Nemirovich-Danchenko, in June 1898, conceived their plan to create their own theatre – the now world-famous Moscow Art Theatre.

THE BOLSHOI THEATRE

On the left of the passage from Dzerzhinsky Square to the former Theatre Square stands a monument to Russia's first master-printer, Ivan Fyodorov, and it was along this part of the Kitai-Gorod that many bookshops sprang up in the early nineteenth century, forming Moscow's famous book market, which survived until the 1920s. The wall then dipped downwards, behind today's Hotel Metropol, and it is here that it has miraculously survived. It can be seen from Theatre Square (now Sverdlov Square, after the first Soviet President, Yakov Sverdlov, 1917–19). This square is the de facto centre of the city, the ever-crowded crossing point for nearby government ministries and offices, hotels and restaurants, and the main department stores. Opposite the wall, across the square, is the Bolshoi Theatre, founded in 1776, and world-famous for its ballet. The present building, with Apollo riding his sun-chariot above the portico, was designed by Bove in 1825 and expanded three decades later by Kavos.

Okhotniy Ryad or Hunters' Row (now Marx Avenue), on the left, was for several centuries famed for its mass of food shops, selling game, poultry, fish and all types of delicacies and provisions. After the Revolution this great food market, once called the 'womb of Moscow', shrank to nothing and in 1935 the Hotel Moskva was erected here, as well as the headquarters of the State Planning Committee, Gosplan. The grey Gosplan colossus all but overshadows the three-storey, azure-white building on the corner of Push-kinskaya, once a Moscow landmark, which from 1784 until the Revolution was the seat of the Assembly of the Nobility and after 1917 became the House of Soviets. Its magnificent dance hall was the scene of the notorious Stalinist trials of the 'enemies of the people' in 1937 and 1938.

Before it reached the Sobakina, or Dog's, Tower of the Kremlin, in front of which is the grave of the Unknown Soldier, a light burning before it night and day, the Kitai-Gorod passed in front of what is now the Lenin Museum

THE GRAVE OF THE UNKNOWN SOLDIER IN THE ALEXANDER GARDEN NEXT TO THE KREMLIN WALL.

(before 1917, the Municipal Council, or City Duma) and the Museum of History. A model of the wall and finds from excavations of the former battlements are on display in the Museum of History, a neo-Russian-style building erected in 1881 in place of the Main Pharmacy, which had housed the first Russian university, opened on 25 January 1755 according to plans drawn up Mikhail Lomonosov. In 1793 a new university building, a distinguished example of Russian classicism designed by Kazakov, was built on the south of Manezhnaya Square (now the Square of the 50th Anniversary of the October Revolution). With the growing number of students and departments, in 1836 another building was erected on the opposite corner of Nikitskaya Street (now Herzen Street), which became known as the 'new university'. Only in 1950, when a vast campus was built around a huge tower in the Lenin Hills, did the name 'new university' get passed on.

The spire-crowned tower of the new university is one of seven 22–24-storeyed structures dating from the late 1940s, when Stalin ordered the construction of such high-

A STATUE OF THE ENCYCLOPEDIST MIKHAIL LOMONOSOV IN FRONT OF THE OLD 'NEW' UNIVERSITY (*top*).

THE CENTRAL RESIDENCE TOWER OF THE NEW UNIVERSITY BUILDING ON THE LENIN HILLS (*above and right*).

rise buildings as visible proof of Russia's ability to over-come the devastation of war. The University, the Ministry of Foreign Affairs and the Ministry of Communications, the Leningrad and the Ukraine hotels, and two apartment buildings – on Kotelnicheskaya Embankment and Vossta-nia Square – now stand as monuments of the Stalin era and examples of its pompous style.

Fifty years after the Kitai-Gorod was completed, it became apparent that another line of fortifications was needed to protect the now much-expanded city and in the late sixteenth century the architect Fyodor Kon was com-missioned to build a new wall. Built of white stone, and tak-ing eight years to complete, it was 10 kilometres (6 miles) long with 27 towers, ten of which had gates. By the late eighteenth century the wall had crumbled into disuse and in the early nineteenth century a belt of boulevards was built over it, the only indication left today of the boundaries of what was called 'White City'.

A trip along the boulevard belt might start from the open-air swimming pool, 'Moskva', on the river bank. This is built on the site of the Cathedral of Christ the Saviour, erected from national funds to commemorate the 1812 vic-tory over Napoleon and destroyed in the early 1930s to make way for the gigantic Palace of the Soviets, which in turn was dismantled when its foundations could not sup-port the weight of its superstructure. From here the Gogol Boulevard leads to a broad square where the Ministry of Defence is located and off which runs Arbat Street, one of the most aristocratic streets in Moscow from the mid-eighteenth to the mid-nineteenth century. In the 1930s and 1940s it was the route to Stalin's home in Kuntsevo and its fearful atmosphere at that time was expressed in Boris Slutsky's poem 'God Rode along Arbat in Five Cars', as

MOSCOW SEEN FROM THE LENIN HILLS (*left*).
THE 'MOSKVA' OPEN-AIR SWIMMING POOL (*above*).

well as Anatoli Rybakov's book *The Children of Arbat*. Today, the street is a lively pedestrian precinct, the domain of artists, street musicians and orators.

Past Suvorovsky Boulevard is Nikitskie Vorota Square, home of the Soviet news agency TASS. Nearby is a small sunken church where the great Russian soldier Alexander Suvorov is buried and, opposite, an imposing white-stone church where Russia's foremost poet, Pushkin, was married. Here too is a fine example of Russian art nouveau architecture, a two-storey town house on Kachalov Street built by Shekhtel for the industrialist Ryabushinsky in 1900 and the home of writer Maxim Gorky on his return from exile in Italy after the Revolution. The house is now the Gorky Memorial Museum.

Tverskoi, the next boulevard, is the oldest and perhaps most famous of all Moscow's boulevards, dating from 1796 and where the *beau monde* gathered to promenade in the early nineteenth century. It includes the old two-storey house rebuilt by Shekhtel at the beginning of the twentieth century for the Smirnov family, of vodka fame, and the Kamerniy Theatre, now called the Pushkin Theatre, opened in 1914. Next to it is the mansion where the author Alexander Herzen was born in 1812 and which appears in Mikhail Bulgakov's novel *The Master and Margarita* as the 'Griboyedov House', headquarters of a writers' organization. Among the Soviet poets and novelists who lived in the house, in fear of arrest, were Osip Mandelstam and Andrei Platonov.

THE ART-NOUVEAU HOUSE OF RYABUSHINSKY, NOW THE GORKY MEMORIAL MUSEUM.

A monument to Pushkin, by Opekushin, was erected in 1880 at the corner of Tverskoi Boulevard and Gorky Street (previously Tverskaya), Moscow's main street, where the bronze figure formed a beautiful silhouette against the sky; but in 1950 it was moved to its present site in Pushkin Square, rather lost against the background of a cinema. The square was renamed in 1937, on the hundredth anniversary of the poet's death, and on 6 June every year people gather here for a festival of poetry to mark his birthday. The beautiful park, with its playing fountains, is laid out on land once occupied by the Strasstnoi (Holy) Monastery.

Within walking distance is the huge, architecturally rather disorganized Mayakovsky Square, named in 1935 after the poet of the revolution Vladimir Mayakovsky, whose bronze statue, by Kibalnikov, stands at the intersection of Gorky Street with one of Moscow's widest avenues, Sadovoye Koltso. The square was previously known as the Old Gates of Triumph and in the eighteenth century was the entrance to the city, where triumphal arches were set up for the arrival of the Russian tsars from St Petersburg to be crowned in Moscow. Today you might arrive from within the capital by Mayakovskaya Metro station, opened in 1938 and perhaps the most attractive of Moscow's spacious underground palaces. It was designed by Dushkin, who was also responsible for Kropotkinskaya station, combining stainless steel, dark-grey marble and red rhodonite, decorated with smalt mosaics by Deineka.

The broad avenue of Sadovoye Koltso, meaning Garden Ring, took its name from the plots of land outside the borders of White City which were originally granted to a special army, the Streltsy – a military corps created in 1550 by Ivan the Terrible – who in return performed guard duty at the Kremlin and marched off to war at the first order. It was the Streltsy who insisted that a further line of fortifica-

tions be built and in 1592 Moscow was encircled by a 15-kilometre (nine mile) earthen rampart, topped by a wooden wall with 52 towers. All traffic to and from the city went through its 12 gates, supervised by guards and customs officers. The Zemlyanoi Val, or Earthen Rampart, was removed in the early nineteenth century to make room for a wide circular road and the vacant plots were planted with orchards, from which the name Garden Ring arose. Both gardens and boulevards were removed before the Second World War, although the name has survived.

The three walls of fortification – the Kitai-Gorod, White City and the Earthen Rampart – formed three concentric circles, with the roads passing through their gates like radii opening into the vast expanses of the country beyond. Ilyinka (Kuibyshev) and Nikolskaya (25th October Anniversary) led north, to Yaroslavl and Vologda; Tverskaya (Gorky Street) led north-west; Arbat Street westwards, to Smolensk; Ordynka Street crossed the Moskva river, going southwards. All these streets were interlinked by narrow, winding lanes, giving Moscow its distinctive layout, very different from the rectilinear plans of St Petersburg; even in the early nineteenth century foreign visitors would be stunned by the length and crookedness of Moscow's streets and lanes, and its innumerable churches.

The spaciousness of the city enabled houses to be built with surrounding gardens, traditionally hidden behind tall wooden fences. Streets would consequently often appear like dirty corridors with wooden walls, only tree-tops visible above them, but there would usually also be several churches and the skyline of a district was often dominated by the high dome of a monastery or convent church. At the

MONUMENTS TO THE POETS MAYAKOVSKY (*top left*) AND PUSHKIN (*top right*).

THE ENTRANCE TO THE KROPOTKINSKAYA METRO STATION.

turn of the nineteenth century, it is said that there were as many as 1,600 churches in Moscow, which is perhaps an exaggeration; it is, however, known for certain that in 1923 there were 610 churches and 42 chapels.

Among the buildings that the State returned to the Church on the thousandth anniversary of Christianity in Russia is one of Moscow's oldest monasteries, the Danilovsky. It was founded in the 1280s by the first independent Moscow prince, Daniil Alexandrovich, who was canonized in the seventeenth century, when his remains were reburied in the monastery. Restored and redecorated, the Danilovsky is today the administrative centre of the Russian Orthodox Church.

In the thirteenth century the monastery served as an advance outpost to warn the Muscovites of the approach of Tartar armies, a service also performed by other monasteries, similarly built as small but strong fortresses, which were spread in a semicircle south of the city. The Simonov Monastery, to the east of the Danilovsky, was the most formidable in the chain, to which the Novospassky Convent – the 'youngest of the guards' – was added in the late fifteenth century. It was built on the bank of the Moskva, next to the tiny Monastery of the Dormition, which became known as the Krutitsky, meaning steep, because of the sharply sloping river bank on which it stood.

The Krutitsky Monastery was of no defence value but it became of significance when the Bishop of the Tartar capital, Saray, moved there in 1460, shortly before the deci-

sive defeat of the Tartars. The Saray bishops had played an important political role since 1262 when the Khan of the Golden Horde had agreed to the appointment of a Russian bishop to administer the thousands of Christians taken prisoner by the Tartars. With the appointment of the patriarch as head of the Russian Orthodox Church in 1590, the Bishop of Saray, now living in the Krutitsky Monastery, was made a metropolitan, charged with the supervision of the Moscow diocese. The monastery acquired lands and wealth with its new status and it was completely rebuilt at the turn of the seventeenth century, becoming famed for its formal gardens with fountains and its impressive entrance. After Catherine the Great secularized many Church estates in the late eighteenth century, the Krutitsky along with various other monasteries ceased to exist but it has now been partially restored, complete with its beautiful tile-work and openwork columns of intertwined vines, and forms a branch of the Museum of History.

The last monastery in the south-eastern chain was the Andronyev, founded by St Andronik, disciple of Russia's most venerated cleric, Sergius of Radonezh, founder of the celebrated monastery in Zagorsk. The great Russian artist, Andrei Rublev, was buried here and the monastery is now a museum in his name containing a remarkable collection of Russian icons. The monastery also boasts the oldest surviving stone structure in Moscow, an almost miraculously beautiful white-stone church built in the early fourteenth century, supposedly with the help of Rublev himself.

THE HOUSE OF THE GREAT RUSSIAN BASS, SCHALIAPIN (*above*).

THE KRUTITSKY MONASTERY (*right*).

TOLSTOY'S HOUSE IN LEO TOLSTOY STREET, WHERE THE WRITER LIVED BETWEEN 1882 AND 1901. IT HAS BEEN PRESERVED AS IT WAS IN HIS LIFETIME.

THE EXTERIOR (*top left*); THE BEDROOM (*top right*); THE DRAWING ROOM (*above left*); THE STUDY (*above right*).

The south-western wing of Moscow was guarded by the Donskoi Monastery and the Novodevichi Convent. The first was built on the battlefield where in 1591 the Tartars who had come to raid Moscow were repulsed by the Russians, never to return, and it was consecrated to the icon of the Holy Virgin of the Don, a national relic which had accompanied the Russian army in its Don River campaign against the Tartars in the late fourteenth century and which again inspired the army in the battle of 1591. The Donskoi Monastery became the burial place for Moscow aristocrats and intellectuals in the eighteenth and nineteenth centuries, among them members of the old princely dynasty, the Golitsyns, the poet and minister Dmitriev (1760–1837), the writer and music critic Odoyevsky (1803–69), the philosopher Chaadayev (1794–1856), the historian Klyuchevsky (1841–1911) and the father of Russian aviation, Zhukovsky (1847–1921). Today the monastery houses museums of architectural history and memorial sculpture, the latter including work by major Russian, French and Italian masons since the eighteenth century.

The well-fortified Novodevichi Convent, founded in 1525, was built near the ford across the Moskva river, guarding possible approaches from Polish or Lithuanian armies, and was appropriately dedicated to the liberation of the old Russian city of Smolensk from Polish occupation. The widow of Ivan the Terrible's son, murdered by his father, became a nun here at the end of the sixteenth century, joined by Irina Godunova following the death of her husband, Tsar Fyodor, in 1598. Boris Godunov her brother, made famous by Mussorgsky's opera of the same name, was elected to the throne and the Novodevichi Convent subsequently enjoyed royal favours. Its riches were used to employ the best artists, jewellers and wood-carvers to decorate its churches and many women of the tsars' families were buried here. Peter I banished his sister Sophia to the convent after her incitement of the Streltsy rebellion in 1698, which was ruthlessly crushed. The rebels were hanged on 300 gallows set up around the convent.

With the capital's move to St Petersburg in 1712, the convent lost its privileged status and from the mid-eighteenth to the mid-nineteenth century it was used as a prison for women. In 1922 a museum of old Russian architecture, painting and applied arts was set up there and the Constructivist artist Tatlin had a studio in the convent's shapely bell tower, the most beautiful of the convent buildings which in their elegance and lightness are a lasting tribute to Russian sixteenth- and seventeenth-century architecture. At the turn of the nineteenth century, a new cemetery was opened near the southern wall of the convent and, after Stalin's wife was buried there in 1932, it became the burial ground of many famous people. As well as prominent generals, Party officials and political leaders, among them Nikita Krushchev, many great scientists and artists are buried here: the composers Skriabin, Prokoviev and Shostakovich; the directors and actors Stanislavsky, Kachalov and Nemirovich-Danchenko; academicians Vernadsky, Fersman and Bakh; and the writers Bulgakov, Ehrenburg and Mayakovsky. To add to its prestige, other famous national figures have been moved from their original burial sites and reburied in the cemetry, including Gogol and Chekhov, and the artists Levitan and Serov.

The monasteries are the key to why Moscow rather than another Russian town became the country's capital. In 1308 the patriarch of Constantinople rejected the metropolitan candidate put forward by Tver, the capital of the biggest Russian principality at that time, and instead appointed the stern monk, Pyotr. Tver, angered by the failure of its protégé, turned away from the new metropolitan and the Moscow prince Ivan Danilovich persuaded Pyotr to settle in his city, which conferred on Moscow the status of the spiritual centre of Russia. After Pyotr's death in 1326 he was buried in the Cathedral of the Dormition, probably built precisely for this purpose, and when shortly afterwards miracles were believed to occur at the metropolitan's tomb, Moscow and north-eastern Russia acquired their national saint and the support of the monasteries. Tver meanwhile had been ransacked by the Tartars and in 1328 the Moscow rulers finally became grand dukes and Moscow the principal city of Russian lands.

Over the following centuries many monasteries and churches were built and the Muscovites became known for their devoutness. Peter the Great curbed the power of the church by abolishing the office of the patriarch in 1703 (established in 1598 and restored in 1917 by the Russian government) and nine years later moved to the newly built capital of St Petersburg, leaving Moscow in danger of becoming an ordinary provincial town. Its citizens asserted their originality and displayed their opposition to the new capital in various ways, from riding about the city in summer in a heavy gilded sledge pulled by many horses, and bringing live sturgeon in huge barrels from the Caspian Sea for a feast lasting many days; to, more seriously, establishing opera and ballet theatres. One Muscovite built a china factory outside Moscow just to satisfy the needs of his household but with strict instructions that his china excel that of the tsar in quality.

In the late eighteenth century fabulous palaces were built in the Moscow countryside which would become

THE NOVODEVICHI CONVENT: THE GATECHURCH OF THE
TRANSFIGURATION (*top left*); WALLS AND TOWERS (*top right and
above*); THE SMOLENSK CATHEDRAL (*right*).

celebrated museums after the Revolution. The Ostankino Palace Museum, which includes the original theatre building complete with stage machinery, is now within the city's boundaries, near the Moscow TV centre with its 325-metre (1066-foot) restaurant tower, but this whole area was once the property of Count Sheremetev, the richest aristocrat in Russia and owner of 210,000 serfs. Nikolai Sheremetev began to build the Ostankino Palace and theatre when he inherited the estate in 1790, and the Sheremetev opera and ballet troupe quickly won renown both in Moscow and St Petersburg. When the count married a beautiful peasant singer, he was ostracized by society and on her death in 1803 he had a grandiose almshouse, designed by Quarenghi, built on Moscow's Garden Ring in her memory.

The Kuskovo estate, also owned by the Sheremetevs, was built over several decades and completed in 1792. Besides the palace itself, it included a church and a hermitage, Italian- and Dutch-style houses, and gardens with a network of ponds and canals, as well as a grotto and huge greenhouse. The summer entertainments here outrivalled those of the Moscow governor-general. Today, the sumptuous rooms of the palace house unique collections of china and ceramics, with fine examples from all the great European factories, among them early Meissen, Chelsea, Wedgewood, Sèvres – including Napoleon's Egyptian service presented to Alexander I in 1808. The riches of the Kuskovo Museum are largely owed to the industrialist, Alexei Morozov, whose rare and extensive collection of

THE VERANDAH OF TCHAIKOVSKY'S HOUSE AT KLIN, 90 KILOMETRES (56 MILES) NORTH-WEST OF MOSCOW WHERE HE LIVED FROM 1885 UNTIL HIS DEATH IN 1893.

Russian china, nationalized along with other private art collections in 1918, was the basis of the museum, of which he became the curator and director until his death in 1934.

The greatest of other avid collectors before the Revolution was the rich businessman Pavel Tretyakov, who founded the Gallery of Russian Art, which he presented to his native city in 1892. Mikhail and Ivan Morozov, of the Morozov family, were also well-known art collectors. Mikhail, the first to collect French art of the late nineteenth to early twentieth century, bequeathed his collection to Moscow before his death in 1903, while his younger brother Ivan continued to acquire French Impressionist works, rivalled only by the Moscow industrialist Sergei Shchukin. The celebrated galleries of these three men were nationalized after the Revolution to form the State Museum of West European Art, housed at first in a mansion on Kropotkinskaya Street which is now the Academy of Arts. Since 1948, the collection has been divided between the Leningrad Hermitage and the Pushkin Museum of Fine Art, opened in 1912.

Philanthropy and patronage of the arts characterized Moscow from the mid-nineteenth century to the early twentieth century, and today, once again, new museums based on private collections are opening in Moscow, as elsewhere. The museums are part of the cultural life of the nation, to be explored along with the capital's innumerable streets and squares, its monasteries, churches, houses and parks, each of which has its own story to tell.

THE DRAWING-ROOM WITH THE PIANO ON WHICH TCHAIKOVSKY COMPOSED. THE HOUSE WAS LOOTED DURING THE WAR BUT HAS BEEN RESTORED.

ZAGORSK
(TROITSA-SERGIEVA LAVRA)

Zagorsk lies some 70 kilometres (43 miles) north of Moscow, on the road leading to Rostov and Yaroslavl, and finally stretching towards Siberia. Today, an hour's journey by the new concrete highway past fields and villages brings you to its festive stone walls with their comely towers, behind which rises the famous Holy Trinity Monastery, founded in the fourteenth century by Sergius of Radonezh and popularly called the Trinity-St Sergius Monastery. The settlement that had arisen around the monastery in the fifteenth century was known as Sergiev Posad, after its founder, until the 1917 Revolution, when it was renamed Zagorsk in honour of a Moscow revolutionary.

This was an area of dense forest in 1355 when Sergius and his elder brother, sons of an impoverished noble family, had come here to live as hermits and built a small wooden church by the bank of a stream. Others, both commoners and noblemen, soon joined them and Russia's first communal monastery was formed, where all work and worship was performed equally in a spirit of Christian brotherhood. Sergius became the monastery's father superior and this intelligent, cultured man sought the patronage of the Moscow princes, whose gifts poured in to enhance the monastery's prestige and wealth. At this period Russia was still living under the Tartar yoke and Sergius used his influence to persuade other Russian princes to back Moscow in fighting the Tartars. After being given Sergius's blessing, the Russian forces finally routed the Tartars in the fierce Battle of Kulikovo. A service of celebration was held at the Holy Trinity Monastery to mark the victory.

The fame and influence of Sergius grew and many new monasteries were founded by his disciples. Whereas only some 30 monasteries were built between 1240 and 1340, nearly 150 were set up in the following century, primarily in the wooded north and north-east of Russia where they became outposts in the development of new territory and important cultural centres. The libraries of such new monasteries as Kirillo-Belozersky and Solovetsky mirrored that of the Holy Trinity, founded by Sergius, who, according to the chronicles, copied books on *beresta*, or specially treated birch-bark, when the monastery was too poor to afford paper or parchment.

In 1382 Sergius of Radonezh died and every year since then people have come to the monastery on 18 July to pay him homage. He was canonized in 1422 and to mark the event the father superior of the monastery, Nikon, decided to build a new stone church to replace the wooden one. Restored in the 1960s, the beautiful Church of the Holy Trinity seems to be cut from a single block of stone; its dazzling white walls are rimmed with lacy ornamentation and its domes sparkle with gold. It is the finest of the three sister churches built at this time, probably by the same team, being more slender and with more sense of upward movement than the white-stone church in the old town of Zvenigorod near Moscow or the Church of the Saviour in Moscow's Spasso-Andronyev Monastery.

The murals inside the church were painted by the famous Andrei Rublev, who was a monk at the Holy Trinity Monastery. Rublev with his assistants also painted all the icons in the grand front iconostasis, including the celebrated 'Trinity', the original of which is now in the Tretyakov Gallery in Moscow. The embroidered cover for the saint's coffin may have been made at the same time as the iconostasis; it portrays Sergius, possibly sketched by Rublev, as a lean-faced man with wide cheekbones and slightly slanting eyes, with a mop of reddish hair and a full beard. The monastery's prestige was such that Russian princes signed their treaties at the coffin of Sergius; prayer services were held in the church before military campaigns; and until the early seventeenth century tsars had their sons baptized here.

After the completion of the church, there was a period of bitter rivalry for the Muscovy throne and no other stone structures were erected in the monastery until later in the

THE BELL TOWER, THE VAST CATHEDRAL OF THE DORMITION AND THE WHITE AND GOLD CHURCH OF THE HOLY TRINITY IN THE TRINITY-ST SERGIUS MONASTERY.

A MONK OUTSIDE THE HOLY TRINITY CHURCH, BUILT ON THE SITE
OF THE GRAVE OF SAINT SERGIUS OF RADONEZH.

century. A new spacious stone refectory was then built in front of the church, where the present belfry stands; the huge vaulted reception hall of the upper storey, supported by a single central pillar, was later made the model for the Hall of Facets in the Kremlin in Moscow. Next to it was built a stone kitchen, which carried less risk of fire than earlier wooden ones, and where luxury dishes were prepared to serve to the monastery's many important guests.

The monastery's wealth enabled it to buy new land and in 1476 a brickwork church was built east of the monastery church by master craftsmen from Pskov. On the roof, supporting a drum crowned by a cupola, six poles were set up with bells hanging between them. Today it is the oldest surviving example of a church belfry.

Major construction work began in the monastery in the mid-sixteenth century, when Ivan the Terrible ordered a strong wall to be built round it, perhaps to provide himself with a place of refuge. Hundreds of local serfs were brought in to labour under master masons in constructing the 1166-metre-long (1275 yards) wall, which was up to three metres (ten feet) thick and included 12 imposing towers. While this powerful fortification was still under construction, a palace for the Tsar was built to the north of the church. New cells for the monks were erected along the new wall and in the now vacant central square a huge new cathedral was begun that was to match the Cathedral of the Dormition in the Moscow Kremlin and was similarly named. The present domes were added in the seventeenth century.

THE HOLY TRINITY CHURCH (*above left*).

A GALLERY OF MONKS' CELLS IN THE MONASTERY (*above*).
THREE OF THE FIVE DAZZLING BLUE AND GOLD DOMES OF THE
CATHEDRAL OF THE DORMITION (*overleaf*).

Ivan's friendly ties with the monastery were, however, broken as his atrocities mounted and were condemned by the monks. Only in 1581 did he visit it again, in remorse at killing his son in a fit of rage – the famous late nineteenth-century painting of this event by Repin is now in Moscow's Tretyakov Gallery. The 5000 roubles that Ivan presented to the monks, requesting them to pray for ever for the soul of his murdered son, went to complete the cathedral, which twenty years later became the burial place of Tsar Boris Godunov (1598–1605) and his family. Two centuries later, the front entrance and the spacious vestibule where Godunov was buried were dismantled and the Godunov family tomb found itself outside the cathedral wall.

The monastery walls were put to a severe test in 1608 when a 30,000-strong Polish army besieged the monastery, but after thirteen months and many bombardments, the Poles were forced to retire, defeated. The cannons seen today in front of the monastery hospital are a reminder of that time. Having withstood the siege, the monastery gave its backing to the new Romanov dynasty, and gifts and favours were again showered on it. By the mid-seventeenth century the monastery boasted more riches than the tsar or the patriarch, including ownership of more than twice the number of serfs in the domains of either of them. It was said by foreigners that Russia recognized three rulers: the sovereign, the patriarch and the treasurer of the Holy Trinity Monastery. After seeing the 'sacral garments and gold and silver utensils studded with gems', the Patriarch of Antioch wrote that 'this monastery has no match not only in the country of Muscovy but anywhere in the world'. Its treasures have almost miraculously survived over the years and can be seen today in the local museum.

With its fabulous wealth, the monastery embarked on a grandiose construction project in the later seventeenth century, a period of country-wide renaissance that saw the birth of a new style of architecture and design – the sumptuous and decorative Moscow baroque. The Holy Trinity fathers first bolstered their fortress by adding two or three tiers to the wall's twelve towers, which were then topped not by the austere pyramidal roofs of the past but by festive pointed caps. The walls were restored and 90 cannons positioned along them, an impressive number when it is considered that the border town of Smolensk, with a wall six times longer, had 106 cannons. Moreover, the monks assembled an arsenal of weapons for 30,000 men.

Diggers, carpenters and masons then went to work near the southern and northern walls, and a remarkable chapel in the form of a tower, 21 metres (69 feet) tall, was erected next to the south-western corner of the cathedral, over a

SEVENTEENTH-CENTURY CANNONS LINED UP IN FRONT OF THE MONASTERY HOSPITAL (*top*).
THE INTERIOR OF THE REFECTORY (*above*).

well of holy water which is popularly reputed to have many healing properties. The festive chapel, consisting of three octahedrons of diminishing size crowned by a cupola, has columns carved with intertwining flowers and grasses, and windows in baroque frames decorated with volutes; its walls are decorated in a multi-coloured chessboard pattern. Another major project was begun almost at the same time: a splendid new refectory, built in 1686. Standing on a high plinth, the building is girdled with a wide gallery and balustrade, and seems to soar above the ground. Large windows, with finely carved columns between them, give light to its 86-metre (282 feet) length and the decorations include a belt of sculptured shells under the roof and the typical chessboard pattern of blue, yellow and red squares on the walls that creates a faceted effect.

For symmetry, a new stone tsar's palace was built near the northern wall to replace the old wooden structure. The two storeys of the building, decorated with chessboard patterns and carved columns, were visually divided by a belt of large coloured tiles, and tiles also framed the double windows of the upper floor. Subsequent rulers rebuilt and redecorated the palace, so that only a few original elements survive, among them the exterior murals and tiles, and some mouldings and beautiful mid-eighteenth-century stoves in two small halls. In 1814 the palace became the Spiritual Academy of the Russian Church, on its transfer from Moscow, and a study building was erected nearby and the service buildings behind were replaced by a library, hospital, dining-room and bath-house. After the October Revolution, the building also accommodated the Seminary, the Church's secondary educational institution, and today some 600 young men study at the Seminary and Academy after undergoing a rigorous selection process – another 900 are students by correspondence.

THE REFECTORY AND, BEFORE IT, THE EIGHTEENTH-CENTURY CHURCH OF ST MICAH.

The last major building period in the monastery was in the mid-eighteenth century. Earlier that century it had been decided to move the Holy Trinity Monastery to the new capital of St Petersburg – and some buildings had already begun to be dismantled before it was realized that the costs of the transferral would be too immense. However, the Empress Anna Ioanovna (1730–40) gave the fathers permission to build a new bell tower of a size and appearance to match the monstery's importance. Working drawings were finally sent from St Petersburg in 1740 and it was to be another 30 years, spanning the reign of Empress Elizabeth (1741–62) and into that of Catherine the Great (1762–96), before the magnificent five-tiered structure was completed. Unfortunately, the massive bronze bell, which weighed 650 tonnes has not survived but the tower, soaring 88 metres (289 feet) into the sky – 6 metres (20 feet) higher than the Kremlin's Ivan the Great Bell Tower – remains as a splendid monument to Russian 'Elizabethan' baroque.

After the bell tower was finished, the mansion of the father superior south of the cathedral, along with some of the monks' cells, was rebuilt when the Metropolitan of Moscow, Platon, made it his residence in the later eighteenth century. Traces of the original sixteenth-century residence can still be seen on the ground floor; to the upper floor were added two formal halls, as well as living quarters. One of these halls, the Tsar's Hall, became a gala reception room when the mansion was redesignated as the residence of the Patriarch of the Russian Church. It was also Metropolitan Platon who in 1792 had an obelisk erected in the centre of the cloister commemorating the monastery's services to Russia. The mission of Sergius of Radonezh continues today and in 1988, during the 1000th anniversary celebrations of Christianity in Russia, it was in the former refectory of the Holy Trinity Monastery that the Council of the Orthodox Church was held. Attending the Council were representatives of all the churches and denominations of the world.

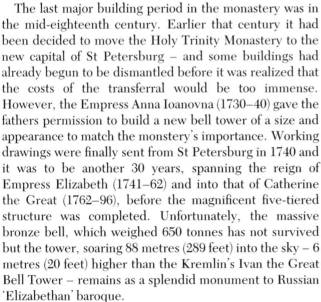

THE REFECTORY'S CARVED AND PAINTED COLUMNS (*left*).
THE DOMES OF THE CHURCH OF THE HOLY TRINITY AND THE
BAROQUE BELL TOWER (*above left*).

THE PINK, EIGHTEENTH-CENTURY FAÇADE OF THE
METROPOLITAN'S CHAMBERS (*above*) – THE PEDIMENT BEARS A
REPRESENTATION OF THE METROPOLITAN'S REGALIA.

ROSTOV THE GREAT

S tanding on a hill overlooking Lake Nero on the road north from Moscow, Rostov seems a vision from a fairytale: a white-walled, towered fortress enclosing red and white buildings with galleries and passageways, and bell towers and churches whose strangely shaped ornamental roofs and cupolas stud the skyline. This ancient town was badly damaged in a whirlwind in 1953 and what is seen today of the old quarter is a restoration to Rostov as it looked in 1727 after a splendid rebuilding programme by the Rostov Metropolitan Jonah. He had been appointed the guardian of the Russian Church on the deposition and exile of the Patriarch Nikon, whose reforms had caused a schism with the 'Old Believers' that still exists today and whose increasing power had finally led Tsar Alexei Romanov to order his trial. For 20 years, until his death in 1690, Jonah supervised the reconstruction of the old, shabby fortress of Rostov to fit the dignity and prestige of his position. The work was completed by his successors by 1727 and the surviving plans were used by the restorers of the 1950s and 1960s.

Many centuries before Jonah, however, Rostov had achieved greatness. It was first mentioned in the chronicles in 862, along with Kiev, Novgorod and other early Russian towns, and it was soon referred to as Rostov the Great because of its wealth and trading importance. Protected from enemy raids by the thick surrounding forests, the town was part of the great trade route to the East, linked by the deep Lake Nero to the Volga, and grew rich trading flax, beeswax and furs in return for precious fabrics, jewellery, arms and spices. It came within the power of the great Kievan principality and in the eleventh century was ruled for a time by Prince Vladimir Monomach.

Missionaries from Kiev built a wooden church here at the end of the tenth century, although Christianity was not easily accepted and in 1071 there was a major uprising, led by two former priests of the pagan gods, in which the church was burnt down and the local bishop, Leontius, was killed. The rebellion was savagely suppressed by troops sent from Kiev and Prince Andrei Bogolyubsky subsequently ordered a stone cathedral to be built on the site of the wooden one, which was to house the tomb of Bishop Leontius whose remains were found in the ashes. Also at the end of the eleventh century, a monastery was established on the eastern outskirts of the city, on what according to legend was a pagan sacred site; it is named after its founder, Avraam, and is one of the oldest in Russia.

THE WALLS AND TOWERS OF THE ROSTOV KREMLIN (*left*).

DENSE BIRCH WOODS ON THE BANKS OF LAKE NERO (*above*). THE FOURTEENTH-CENTURY MONASTERY OF OUR SAVIOUR AND ST JACOB OUTSIDE ROSTOV (*overleaf*).

Many scholars, artists and craftsmen were attracted to the prosperous medieval city, which became known for its highly decorative yet human style of icon painting – now referred to as the Rostov-Suzdal school – and for its learning and monastic book production. The Grigorievsky Monastery, set on the edge of the lake near the prince's palace, was famous for its school and library, and Rostov was the home of several celebrated chroniclers. Among them were the fifteenth-century writer Epiphany the Wise, who wrote the first life of St Sergius of Radonezh, founder of the great Holy Trinity Monastery in Zagorsk and who himself came from Rostov; and Princess Maria, whose husband and father both met their deaths at the hands of the Tartars in the thirteenth century and who founded a nunnery on the east of Rostov where she wrote a chronicle of the Russian princes martyred in the Tartar struggle.

In the fifteenth century another famous chronicle was produced in Rostov, detailing the history of Russia and written either by Bishop Vassian of Rostov himself or on his orders. This influential bishop persuaded Tsar Ivan III in 1480 to face the Tartar horde of Ahmat-Khan, then outside Moscow, in what became known as the 'Stand on the Ugra'. After three weeks the Tartars retreated and the liberation of northern Russia, already largely achieved a hundred years before at the Battle of Kulikovo, was now made final and Russia ceased to pay the humiliating annual tribute to her long-standing enemy.

It was Bishop Vassian who decided to build a new cathedral in Rostov, replacing the previous stone and brick construction which itself was a rebuilding of the first stone cathedral and which had managed to survive the Tartar sieges of the thirteenth and fourteenth centuries and many fires. Craftsmen were ordered to model the new cathedral on Moscow's great Cathedral of the Dormition and a faithful provincial imitation was produced. Two centuries later Metropolitan Jonah repaired the cathedral, had new frescos painted and ordered a new iconostasis – made in the mid-eighteenth century by skilled wood-carvers. Unfortunately, the seventeenth-century frescos were repainted with oils in the recent restoration. The remains of the chapel containing the eleventh-century tomb of Bishop Leontius were discovered near the southern wall of the cathedral during excavation work in 1884 and subsequent excavations have revealed the foundations of the first two stone and brick cathedrals and fragments of the majolica floor tiles dating back to the twelfth century.

The cathedral, the bishop's residence, the Grigorievsky Monastery and the prince's palace had been the main buildings forming the centre of medieval Rostov and when

THE CHURCH OF ST GREGORY THE THEOLOGIAN – PART OF THE
OLD GRIGORIEVSKY MONASTERY (*top*).
DOMES OF THE CATHEDRAL OF THE DORMITION (*above*).

Jonah drew up his reconstruction plans in the late seventeenth century, he decided not to disrupt this ensemble. Time had destroyed the prince's palace, disbanded the monastery and changed the surrounding land into a vast orchard, but by restoring some old buildings and erecting new ones in a common architectural style, he created the beautiful Rostov Kremlin that is seen today.

By the south-eastern corner of the repaired cathedral, a four-arched bell tower was built which housed 13 bells, each chosen and named by Jonah himself, who was a connoisseur and lover of bell-ringing. The deep voice of the largest bell, weighing 32 kilos (70 pounds) and named 'Sisoi' after Jonah's father, could be heard 18 kilometres (11 miles) away. These bells have been restored and their peals recorded for modern lovers of early bell music.

A low stone wall encloses three sides of the square on which the cathedral stands, while the strong defensive wall on the south side is part of the wall built to guard the residence of Metropolitan Jonah. With its loop-holes, crenellations and 11 towers, this wall appears threatening, but the coquettish baroque crowns of the towers, the patterned surrounds of the loop-holes and the sumptuous gates into the courtyard proclaim equally its symbolic purpose. Through the 'Metropolitan Gate' on the north side, the spiritual lord passed from his apartments into the town's main church; while the tsar passed through the 'Prince's Gate' on the west side into the main courtyard of the residence. Gatechurches emphasized their importance.

The five-domed Church of the Resurrection was built above the northern gate and the Church of St John the Evangelist above the western gate. They have galleries running along three sides and each façade is divided into three parts and crowned by a small triangular pediment. Narrow, elegant drum vaults support the swollen onion domes. Instead of the usual iconostases, both churches have stone screens dividing the sanctuary from the nave, as was the early Christian custom, and the walls and every other available surface are painted with bright frescos. The most interesting frescos are found in St John the Evangelist, where the life and deeds of Avraam, founder of the eleventh-century monastery in Rostov, are depicted on the three upper tiers of the wall and there is the artist's impression of the Rostov Kremlin as it would have appeared in the seventeenth century.

Both the metropolitan's mansion and the prince's palace face inwards onto a vast central square with a large pool. The recently restored prince's palace combines a variety of styles in two-storeyed structures, each with its own roof – a compositional design that was fashionable in the seventeenth-century. The highly decorated royal apartments and reception halls were on the second floor, reached by a wide staircase that gave straight onto the street via a lavish porch. The grandest receptions took place in the vast Red Chamber, made light by its 11 large windows, and it was this beautiful hall that gave its name to the whole palace, which is still known today as the Red Palace.

THREE OF THE THIRTEEN BELLS WHICH HANG IN THE BELL TOWER.

THE BELL TOWER AND THE CHURCH OF THE RESURRECTION BUILT OVER THE 'METROPOLITAN GATE' (*above*).
THE CHURCH OF ST JOHN THE EVANGELIST (*overleaf*).

THE CHURCH OF ST JOHN (*top*) AND
WEATHER VANES ON PORCH OF THE RED
CHAMBER (*above*).

Although more modest in appearance, the metropolitan's palace was built on three floors, the first – constructed in the sixteenth century – and third housing the servants' and service quarters. The metropolitan's private apartments and reception halls on the second floor were connected to a spacious dining-room and the Chapel of Christ the Saviour. This small church, set high off the ground, looks like a graceful donjon, with only its gilded dome and three apses showing that it is a house of prayer. Indicative of Jonah's status and ambitions, there are eight steps rather than the usual two or three from the nave to the solium – the raised area in front of the iconostasis where the priest stands during services. At the end of the eighteenth century, the residence of the metropolitan was rebuilt in provincial classical style and this is how it is seen today, having lost much of its earlier charming individuality.

Also facing the square is the Church of the Virgin Hodegetria (Virgin of Smolensk), which is decorated in painted chessboard patterns and differs greatly in outline from all the other nearby churches. It is but one of the many other historic buildings to be enjoyed in Rostov; as you explore the ancient galleries and passages, look into the small narrow yards and up to the high narrow chimneys crowned with tent-like covers with black streamers. From the Red Palace, a special corridor leads out onto the fortress wall and you can stroll along its top to the next building, enter the round echoing rooms of the fortress towers or gaze down at the waters of the lake. Perhaps too you might buy a piece of many-coloured enamel jewellery, based on the enamelling art first practised in Rostov at the beginning of the eighteenth century and for which this charming and historic town is again famed.

THE DECORATIVE, MANY-COLOURED FAÇADE OF THE CHURCH OF THE VIRGIN HODEGETRIA AND, BEHIND IT, THE DOMES OF THE CATHEDRAL OF THE DORMITION.

THE PAINTED CHESSBOARD PATTERNS THAT COVER THE WALLS OF THE CHURCH OF THE VIRGIN HODEGETRIA (*right*).

TRADITIONAL PAINTED PEASANT HOUSES IN ROSTOV; THE
WINDOWS AND EVES ORNAMENTED WITH INTRICATELY CARVED
WOODEN BOARDS.

YAROSLAVL

In the eleventh century, Yaroslav, Prince of Rostov and later the celebrated Prince of Kiev, founded a Christian fortress at the point where the River Kotorosl flowed into the Volga, thus guarding Rostov's trade waterway. Legend has it that the prince went out hunting and killed a very large bear. To commemorate this event he founded a fortified town, Yaroslavl, and the slaughtered bear became a symbol of the city. In fact, the truth is much more prosaic. The Finno-Ugric settlement that had long existed on the spot was destroyed, along with the she-bear that the inhabitants worshipped, but the town named after Yaroslav still features a bear on its coat-of-arms. Over the following centuries Yaroslavl grew in size and strength, for a while even becoming a small independent principality, but after the hardships suffered under the Tartars and the internecine wars, it sought protection under the wings of the powerful principality of Moscow.

For a brief period in 1612 Yaroslavl became the Russian capital after Moscow and many other Russian towns had fallen to Polish troops. An army to repel the invaders was gathered under two of Yaroslavl's citizens, Prince Dmitry Pozharsky and the merchant Kuzma Minin (a monument to them is in Moscow's Red Square), and after its success Yaroslavl became fired by ambitions to dispute Moscow's supremacy. The city was no less rich, was famed for its fine craftsmen and could equal the capital in the beauty and number of its churches and stone buildings. Some 20 historical buildings survive from this period of rivalry and, unusually, it was the merchants rather than the nobility who commissioned the fine new churches.

The first wealthy merchant to build his own church was Nadeya Sveteshnikov, who became the supplier to the royal court after his support of Mikhail, the first tsar of the Romanov dynasty. He traded all over Russia and had great warehouses in Archangelsk in the north, in Astrakhan in the south, in Pskov in the west, in Siberia, and in the distant east in Yakutsk. In 1613, Mikhail gave Sveteshnikov the title of 'the Muscovite merchant of the Tsar'. Sveteshnikov had used his money to help Mikhail Romanov to gain power and now the Tsar in turn gave him the right to buy goods for 'the Tsar's private usage'. A surviving document tells how when the merchant came to Moscow, he was always present at the Tsar's dinner table and at that of the Patriarch. His austere, five-domed church, dedicated to St Nicholas, the patron of merchants and sailors, was built in 1622 on the bank of the Volga and, with its raised floor or *podklet* and two-storeyed gallery, served also as a storehouse and more importantly as a meeting place to discuss business and political affairs. For his private use Sveteshnikov built a chapel against the northern wall, with a separate entrance; its festive frescos contrasted with the solemn decorations of the majestic St Nicholas and included two portrayals of dishonest, greedy monks which were a scarcely veiled attack on the ancient Spassky Monastery and its attempts to take over lands belonging to Yaroslavl's citizens. Finally, the monastery was forced to give way. At the end of the nineteenth century, Count Musin-Pushkin found the manuscript of the *Lay of Igor's Host* in the Spassky Monastery. This masterpiece of early Russian literature, written about 1140, is today known through Borodin's opera *Prince Igor*.

After the completion of St Nicholas, the two merchant brothers, Druzhina and Gury Nazariev, began the construction of the Church of the Nativity, completed in 1644 by Gury's sons. The varied architecture of the church itself, the chapels, gallery, passages, clock tower and bell tower, combines attractively and produces interesting effects of light and shade. Probably influenced by the family's Asian trade and passion for the East, the exterior of the church was decorated with strips of sparkling coloured tiles, their first use in this way in Russia. Along the door of the cathedral, eleven coloured chronicles document its construction. For the first time in Russian history, the ordinary merchants did not fear to put their names here as the nobles had long been accustomed to do. Thus the newly-born third estate began to assert itself.

The most beautiful church in Yaroslavl was begun three years later, built by the richest merchants of all, the brothers Anikey and Nifanty Skripin, who controlled the vastly lucrative Siberian fur trade. It was not by mere chance that Anikey headed the struggle with the Spassky Monastery for the right to own land in the centre of Yaroslavl. When at last the Tsar and the Patriarch finally decided the affair to the citizens' advantage, the Patriarch presented the Skripins with a sacred relic, a fragment of Christ's cope. It was a sign of greatest respect. The majestic, five-domed Church of the Prophet Elijah, with two-storeyed galleries running along three of its sides, is complemented by a graceful, octagonal bell tower on its north-west and by similarly graceful chapels on the south-east and north-east corners. The church's wonderful frescos, by three teams of artists, were painted 30 years later. Based on the life of Elijah and his disciple Elisha, they depict details of Russian life with a freshness and authenticity that makes them almost an illustrated encyclopedia. There is a scene where a woman in labour is being taken care of and a child is being bathed, and scenes of ploughing and harvesting. Their charm also lies in their pristine condition – they have never been repainted, only carefully washed. At the same time the gallery was decorated with a wide band of tiles scattered with precious stones.

Colourful tiled decoration became a distinguishing feature of Yaroslavl's churches and although the town's architecture became more stiff and austere after the capital moved to St Petersburg in 1711 and Yaroslavl gave up its competition with Moscow, ceramic decoration became even more lavish, with almost fantastic effects of multi-coloured garlands and necklaces wound round walls, columns and domes. The most famous example of the art, fully exploiting all the possibilities, is the big 'dressed' window of the potters' own Church of St John Chrysostom.

When Catherine the Great ordered in 1778 that the centres of all major provincial towns be rebuilt in neo-classical style, Yaroslavl underwent a major reconstruction. The Church of Elijah the Prophet became the focus of the town's new central square, with new streets and squares laid out beyond it. Dignified late eighteenth-century official buildings now line two sides of the central square. In each one of the adjoining streets there are certain houses which differ greatly from all the other buildings. They gaze out on the world through their many windows with an air of self-respect and importance. Such

buildings in the early nineteenth-century neo-classical style demand special attention. For the most part they were constructed with wood, but then plastered to look as though they were made of large blocks of limestone. They are smaller than the palaces and mansions of Moscow and St Petersburg, but even in their details they tend to imitate them. It was here, in these cosy drawing-rooms, with old mahogany furniture, cushions embroidered with beads, and young ladies' albums with touching poems that, at the beginning of the nineteenth century, Russian belle-lettres and poetry were born.

The atmosphere can be recaptured by wandering through the old city and stopping by the house that once belonged to the Nikitins (6 Svoboda Street), or the mansions of the merchants Lazarev (in what is now Komsomolskaya Street), or the three-storeyed building at 61 Kooperativnaya Street and the house where the Association of Physicians is now located on the bank of the Volga (17 Volga Embankment).

At this time the now unnecessary defensive earthworks were levelled and replaced by boulevards, and in 1825 the steep grassy slope down to the Volga was given a more impressive frontage, with a tree-lined promenade created along the top, giving fine views over the Volga. This great waterway, the longest river in Europe, is now connected by canals with the Baltic, the White Sea, and the Azov and Black Seas, and has helped define the modern development of Yaroslavl as an industrial centre.

Old Yaroslavl is not forgotten in the active modern life of the town and the recent decision to restore the former Tolgsky Monastery, founded at the beginning of the fourteenth century at the mouth of the small River Tolga, was greatly welcomed. The first wooden church was erected on the very place where a miracle-working icon of Mary the Mother of God had been 'found'. For a long time the monastery was very poor. The first stone building appeared here only in the later sixteenth century – the main monastic church was erected by order of Ivan the Terrible. The monastery finally began to prosper when the first Romanovs were on the throne. It was then that the stone dining-room and church, and the walls, the towers and the ceremonial entrance – the Sacred Gates – were erected. At the same time the church built by Ivan the Terrible was replaced by a vast new church with a massive bell tower. The last stone buildings to be added to the monastery were hospital wards with their own adjoining church. The large complex of impressive seventeenth-century buildings, will be handed over to a nunnery, and its hospital will once again be open to the citizens of Yaroslavl.

THE RUSSIAN EMPIRE

PALACE SQUARE IN LENINGRAD
AND THE ALEXANDER COLUMN.

LENINGRAD
(ST PETERSBURG, PETROGRAD)

For just over two hundred years the beautiful city of St Petersburg, founded by Peter the Great in 1703 as an outlet to the Baltic Sea, was the capital of the Russian Empire; after the beginning of the First World War it was at first renamed Petrograd to erase the German association, and then in 1924 Leningrad. The tsars of Muscovy had long recognized that without access to the Baltic, no large Russian state could exist and even in the late sixteenth century Ivan the Terrible had tried unsuccessfully to push through to its shores. The chief aim of young Peter, influenced by his education in the West when he had even worked in the Dutch shipyards at Zaandam, had been to open the 'doors to the sea' and he envisaged a Russian navy and a great Baltic port with English, French, Dutch and German ships standing in its wharfs.

In the late seventeenth century the Swedes still held all the outlets to the Baltic Sea but in April 1703 Russian troops captured the Swedish garrison at the point where the River Neva flows into the Gulf of Finland. On 27 May, the foundations of a fortress, called Sankt-Peter-Burgh, were laid on a small island – only 750 metres long and 360 wide (820 × 390 yards) – in the mouth of the Neva, but around it were over a hundred other islands on which Peter's dream city could rise. The hurriedly chosen site, low-lying and marshy, was subject to floods every autumn from the swollen waters of the Neva but the impatient Peter was not to be deterred from his building project. Countless serfs were brought in as labourers and it is estimated that over 100,000 people died during the first ten years of St Petersburg's construction. Brick factories were established and in 1706 work started on rebuilding the original fortress, followed by a replacement for the wooden church of St Peter and St Paul and the Tsar's residence – originally a two-roomed house.

Foreign ambassadors were informed that Russia had a harbour on the Baltic and rewards of gold were promised to the first three ships to anchor there. With Sweden's defeat at Poltava in 1709, Russia was established as a great power and that year St Petersburg was officially proclaimed the capital. It had been decided to build the main square of the new city on the spit of Vasilievsky Island, where the first Governor-General of St Petersburg, Prince Menshikov, had already constructed his wooden residence. The Prince's house was subsequently rebuilt in stone and, now carefully restored, it gives a strong feel of life in early eighteenth-century St Petersburg.

Peter himself took up residence in the city in 1712 and brought in the Italian-Swiss architect, Domenico Tressini, as his principal court architect. Peter envisaged his capital as a new Amsterdam: a harbour and shipbuilding city; the streets would be waterways, with the Neva as the main avenue. The unusual grid layout of Vasilievsky Island reflects this plan, with three broad avenues running east to west intersected at right angles by streets drawn north to south. Excavations started in 1717 but the work was not completed in Peter's lifetime and, despite the plans, St Petersburg expanded on the mainland side. Soon after Peter's death the canals began to be filled in and streets constructed.

It took a quarter of a century before the red-brick walls of the mighty Peter and Paul Fortress – the main link in the defences against Swedish attack – were completed. Later in the eighteenth century the southern side of the fortress, opposite the imperial palace, was clothed in granite after Catherine II had supposedly expressed her dislike of the colour of the fortress walls, reflected blood-red in the waters of the Neva. During its long history the fortress has never fired a shot in anger but it quickly became a prison for important political offenders, a Russian equivalent to the Bastille. Here in 1718 Peter the Great's son Alexei was incarcerated, after opposing his father's reforms. Tried for treason, he was sentenced to death at Peter's insistence and was secretly asphyxiated in one of the fortress's cells. Peter afterwards gave orders for a medal to be struck to

commemorate 'the re-establishment of calm' and commissioned Tressini to erect a building for the Secret Chancellery, the organization charged with investigating anti-government activities. Over the next two centuries, many writers and intellectuals, revolutionaries and assassins, military and political leaders accused of crimes against the state, were locked up in the fortress; among the last prisoners were the ministers of the Provisional Government, in November 1917. Today the fortress is a museum of the city's history, where the prison cells, including that which accommodated the writer Maxim Gorky in 1905, can be visited, along with the Commandant's House where the republican idealists who were involved in the Decembrist military revolt of 1825 were tried.

In the centre of the fortress rises the tall, golden spire of the Cathedral of St Paul and St Peter, designed by Tressini and built in 1714–25 on the site of the original wooden church. In keeping with Peter I's reforming enthusiasm and Western ideas, the stone cathedral differed markedly from the traditional Russian church. There was no eastern apse, enormous windows flooded the interior with light and, instead of a narthex, a tall, thin bell tower abutted the western wall. Its sharp spire was crowned by an unusual weather-vane in the form of an angel holding a cross. On Peter's orders, the cathedral became the burial place of Russia's rulers and in the nineteenth century a large chapel was built onto the northern side to accommodate a tomb for members of the royal family. According to legend, the tomb of Alexander I is empty, for he is supposed to have secretly abdicated, rather than died, in 1825 and become a religious hermit, tormented by guilt for his part in the assassination of his father, Paul I.

The fortress, with the cathedral, marked the centre of the city and under the protection of its guns, directly across the Neva, was built the imperial palace, the second symbol of St Petersburg's power. The Winter Palace seen today is the fifth to stand on the spot and, with its extensions, is now the State Hermitage, one of the biggest art galleries in the world. The original, small, wooden Winter House was replaced in 1711 with a stone structure, finished just in time for the wedding in February 1712 of Peter and his second wife, Catherine I. Four years later work began on a new, much grander palace, appropriate for the ruler of an enormous empire. The façade of the white and gold square building, with galleries opening out onto an inner court-yard, stretched almost 70 metres (230 feet) along the Neva, while the quarters at the rear looked onto the River Moika. It was in this palace that Peter died in 1725 and Catherine I continued to rule the country for the next two years.

THE WALLS OF THE PETER AND PAUL FORTRESS THAT LOOK ONTO THE WINTER PALACE ARE FACED WITH GRANITE.

A DOUBLE-HEADED IMPERIAL EAGLE (*top*) SURMOUNTS ST PETER'S GATE WHICH LEADS INTO THE FORTRESS (*centre*).

THE CATHEDRAL SPIRE (*above*).
AN EIGHTEENTH-CENTURY PAVILION, BUILT IN THE FORTRESS TO HOUSE PETER THE GREAT'S BOAT (*left*).

In the 1730s the Italian architect Bartolomeo Rastrelli built a fourth Winter Palace for Empress Anna, at the western end of Peter's palace. This stood for some twenty years before Rastrelli designed another palace on its foundations for Empress Elizabeth. She died in 1762, the year of its completion, and Catherine II became its sole mistress until her death in 1796. Rastrelli's Winter Palace is one of the most outstanding examples of baroque architecture in the world. Occupying 10,441 square metres (12,487 square yards), the enormous, three-storeyed structure consists of four sections, each with its own inner courtyard, connected by galleries containing suites of formal rooms on the first floor; a large courtyard in the shape of a cross forms the centre of the complex. The elaborately ornamented façades of the four sections are each unique and every detail contributes to the grandeur of the building. The turquoise of the walls contrasts with the white of the columns and the gold of their capitals, and with the stucco window mouldings. Along the edge of the great stretch of roof were originally 80 white stone statues of ancient gods, which were replaced in 1892 by the present bronze statutes. A terrible fire in 1837 destroyed much of the interior, which has 1,050

THE WINTER PALACE.

rooms, 1,945 windows, 1,886 doors and 117 staircases. Of the original interior structures that have been preserved, the best is probably the Grand Staircase, also known as the Ambassadorial Staircase, on the northern side.

Catherine II's favourite architect was the Italian Giacomo Quarenghi, whom she commissioned to build the Hermitage Theatre in 1782–5 on the eastern side of the palace, on the site of Peter the Great's Winter Palace. It was only in 1985, when it was decided to restore the theatre, that it was discovered that Quarenghi had not demolished the old palace interior but 'placed' his theatre

in it. Behind the fine river façade designed by Quarenghi in neo-classical style, the entire ground floor of Peter I's palace was preserved and its galleries and several of its halls can be seen today. Extensions added to the eastern side of the palace in the late eighteenth century were to house Catherine II's rapidly expanding collection of European art, but as the imperial collection grew, these quarters too became overcrowded, particularly when the splendid collections of Russian aristocrats were added after the 1917 Revolution. It was then that the whole palace complex was made into a museum and renamed the State Hermitage.

DETAILING ON THE EXTERIOR OF THE
WINTER PALACE.

THE AMBASSADORIAL STAIRCASE IN THE WINTER PALACE
DESIGNED BY RASTRELLI.

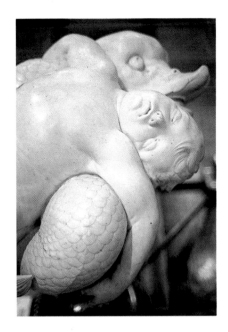

SCULPTURES IN THE HERMITAGE (*top*); 'DEAD BOY ON A DOLPHIN'
BY LORENZO LORENZETTO (*left*); THE TAURIDE VENUS (*centre*); A
DOUBLE-SIDED ROMAN HEAD (*right*).

A FIRST-CENTURY STATUE OF THE EMPEROR OCTAVIAN AUGUSTUS,
SEATED ON A THRONE WITH A SCEPTRE IN ONE HAND AND
WINGED VICTORY IN THE OTHER (*above*).

The building of Peter I's fortress and Winter Palace was immediately followed by the Admiralty, the shipyard that was central to Peter's dreams of a harbour capital. In his determination to foster love for the navy, without which he realized that Russia would have no future, Peter personally gave boating lessons on the Neva on Sundays for every prominent citizen; truants had to pay large fines. Significantly, too, he decreed that all buildings in St Petersburg were to have their main entrances facing the water. The Admiralty was obviously crucial to Peter's plans and the original wooden structure, with twelve shipbuilding slips, was defended by tall ramparts and bastions, and surrounded by a deep moat, with additional protection provided by the gun-cover of the fortress across the water. In the 1720s the wooden Admiralty was rebuilt in stone by the architect Ivan Korobov, who had studied in Holland and Belgium, and he emphasized the main entrance by adding a three-tiered tower whose narrow gilded spire was topped by a miniature ship.

The splendid neo-classical Admiralty building seen today was a rebuilding, keeping to Korobov's original layout, by Adrian Zakharov in 1806–15. The dilapidated U-shaped building standing next to the elegant Winter Palace in the very heart of the city had a straight façade stretching for 400 metres (440 yards), with wings 170 metres (185 yards) long, and Zakharov succeeded in making it look as majestic as the neighbouring palace. He avoided monotony by varying the architectural elements in the façade – projections, columned porticoes and rows of windows – and the imposing effect of the enormous building is further augmented by bas-reliefs, sculptures and the stately tower over the main entrance, which retains the tall gold spire with its ship in full sail from the old Admiralty. It was widely believed that the ship's hold was filled with gold coins from the time of Peter I, put there as ballast, but hopes were dashed when restoration work after World War II revealed that there was no treasure.

On the opposite bank from the Admiralty stand the Twelve Colleges, built in Dutch baroque style by Tressini in 1722–32 as government ministries and intended to form the western boundary of St Petersburg's main square. They stand shoulder to shoulder, deliberately alike, for Peter wished to stress the ministries' equal ranking. In front of the buildings, occupied since the nineteenth century by the University, government decrees and announcements were posted, on the spot where the statue of the scientist and scholar Mikhail Lomonosov now stands.

The great temple building dramatically sited at the tip of Vasilievsky Island was erected in 1810–16 as the home of

THE ADMIRALTY (*top*). THE ENTRANCE IS DECORATED WITH A DOUBLE-HEADED IMPERIAL EAGLE (*above*).

St Petersburg's Stock Exchange; it is now a museum of Russian naval history. On two promontories in front of it stand the immense twin Rostral Columns, which act as beacons, while below, the granite embankment sweeps down to the water. This stunning ensemble was created by the French-born architect Thomas de Thomon, who was killed when he fell from a scaffold while working on the reconstruction of the Bolshoi Theatre (now the Kirov Opera and Ballet) in St Petersburg, which had been badly damaged by fire in 1811.

The golden spire of the Admiralty, visible from afar, marks the point where Leningrad's three main thoroughfares meet: Nevsky Prospect, Srednaya Perspectiva (now Dzerzhinsky Street) and Voznesenskaya Perspectiva (now Maiorov Prospect). Nevsky Prospect was named after the Russian saint and thirteenth-century military hero, Alexander Nevsky, who had triumphed over Sweden and the Teutonic knights in 1240 and 1241. Recognizing that his capital had to have sacred relics, of which Moscow could boast many, Peter I had Nevsky's sacred remains brought to St Petersburg and built the splendid new Alexander Nevsky Monastery further up on the bank of the Neva to house them. Construction of the monastery went on throughout the eighteenth century and it was the burial place for many members of the royal family and distinguished Russian citizens. Here can be found the graves of the military leader Alexander Suvorov, the scholar Mikhail Lomonosov, the architects Giacomo Quarenghi, Adrian Zakharov and Carlo Rossi, the composers Modest Moussorgsky and Peter Tchaikovsky, and the writers Ivan Krylov and Fyodor Dostoyevsky.

THE OLD STOCK EXCHANGE, NOW A MUSEUM OF RUSSIAN NAVAL HISTORY, ON VASILIEVSKY ISLAND (*above*).

THE ROSTRAL COLUMNS (*top*) STAND IN FRONT OF THE EXCHANGE.

THE ALEXANDER NEVSKY MONASTERY (*left*) AND GRAVES IN THE
MONASTERY CEMETERY (*above*).

The monastery was not yet a reality when the road to it, the city's principal street of Nevsky Prospect, began to be laid out in 1712, using Swedish prisoners as forced labourers. On its completion, tolls were charged and in 1721, with the money collected, lamp-posts were put up every 100 metres (110 yards) along the route, with lamplighters hired to light them each evening and extinguish them in the morning. The avenue runs straight as an arrow from the Admiralty to what is now known as Moscow Station, where it met the road from Novgorod and thereafter was named Staro-Nevsky or Old Nevsky. In the eighteenth and nineteenth centuries, Nevsky Prospect became the strolling haunt of St Petersburg society. Both sides of the broad street were lined with fashionable shops, coffee-houses, confectioners and booksellers. It assumed a life of its own and many Russian authors, in particular Gogol, wrote of it.

Today Nevsky Prospect remains the heart of the city's life, particularly beautiful in the quiet of the early morning when the buildings can be more easily admired. First, however, comes Palace Square in front of the Winter Palace at the centre of Leningrad. In the 1730s, the square was bounded on the eastern side by the enormous stables of the Guards, built of wood, with the houses of the townspeople forming a broad curve to the south and stretching as far as Nevsky Prospect. Among these buildings was the Hotel London, where the ballerina Gertrude Rossi and ballet master Charles Lepique probably stayed in 1785 when they performed at St Petersburg's Bolshoi Theatre. It was Gertrude's son Carlo Rossi, born in Naples but brought up in Russia, who was commissioned in 1819 by Alexander I to lay out a 'correct' square before the Winter Palace and erect buildings for the General Staff and Ministries of Foreign Affairs and Finance.

Rossi's stately neo-classical buildings followed the sweeping curve of the former townspeoples's homes. The General Staff stretched from Nevsky Prospect to the centre

PALACE SQUARE: LOOKING FROM THE WINTER PALACE PAST THE
ALEXANDER COLUMN TO THE ARCH LINKING THE GENERAL STAFF
BUILDING WITH THE MINISTRY OF FOREIGN AFFAIRS.

of the square and the Ministry of Foreign Affairs followed the same arc on the eastern side. The Ministry of Finance was built along the River Moika, bending south at the square and intersecting Nevsky Prospect a little further down. The grand sweep and majestic classicism of Rossi's buildings make a worthy frame for the ornate baroque façade of Rastrelli's palace, with the most beautiful effect created by Rossi's triumphal arch linking the General Staff building and the Ministry of Foreign Affairs. This vast monument to Napoleon's defeat in the War of 1812 is crowned by a winged statue of Victory driving a bronze chariot drawn by six horses. When it was being assembled, sceptics thought that the arch would not withstand the weight and Rossi refuted them by standing underneath as the statue was installed.

Alexander I died in 1825, four years before work on the square was completed. He was succeeded by Nikolai I, who commissioned the monument commemorating the Russian victory over France which stands in the centre of the square. It was designed by the Frenchman Auguste Montferrand, who had directed the rebuilding of the vast Cathedral of St Isaac in St Petersburg. Unveiled in 1834, the 25-metre-tall (82 feet) granite column, topped by an angel (with the face of Alexander I) holding a cross, rests securely on its pedestal by the sheer force of its weight: even heavy shelling during the German bombardment of Leningrad in World War II could not shake it.

Palace Square opens onto an ensemble of magnificent central squares. The present boulevard in front of the Admiralty was built in the late nineteenth century and in Rossi's design the rounded space before the Winter Palace flowed into the rectangular Admiralty Square, which led past the ornate Cathedral of St Isaac to the small but stately portico of the Manège, originally the Horseguards' Riding School, designed by Quarenghi in 1800–4, which is now the city's main exhibition hall.

Between the cathedral and the Neva to the north lies another large square – Senate Square (Decembrists' Square) – bounded by a wing of the Admiralty to the east and the vast Senate and Synod buildings to the west. The latter were built to designs by Rossi in the 1830s, with a more elaborate façade than the buildings on Palace Square, and with a magnificent arch joining them decorated with statues symbolizing Justice, Truth, Impartiality and other virtues.

Magnificent too is the rounded and colonnaded corner of the Senate facing the Neva, which reveals a view of the river and the bank beyond, with its group of impressive buildings: the Academy of Arts; the palace of St Petersburg's first Governor-General and intimate of Peter I, Alexander Menshikov; the Academy of Sciences; and the

Cabinet of Curios, Russia's first history and ethnography museum, founded by Peter I. A statue of the reforming emperor, depicted on horseback, stands on Senate Square facing the Neva. It was the work of the French sculptor Etienne-Maurice Falconet, friend of the encyclopedist Diderot, and its symbolism was celebrated by Pushkin in his poem 'The Bronze Horseman'. The monument was the gathering point for the Decembrist military uprising on 14 December 1825, which was quickly crushed by the forces loyal to Nikolai I and its starry-eyed idealist leaders were either hanged or exiled.

Returning to the beginning of Nevsky Prospect, near the point where it crosses the Moika, we find on its northern side a building with loggia-style porticoes at the corners

MASSIVE GRANITE COLUMNS, 17 METRES (56 FEET) HIGH FORM
THE PORTICOES OF THE CATHEDRAL OF ST ISAAC.

THE INTERIOR OF THE CATHEDRAL.

which now houses an antiquarian bookshop and The Literary Café. Originally the home of Vice-Admiral Cornelius Cruys, intimate of Peter I, in the 1830s it became a fashionable patisserie and it was from here that the poet Pushkin set out in 1837 to fight his fatal duel. The cinema across the street occupies the site of a large wooden house that was the temporary residence of Empress Elizabeth in the mid-eighteenth century. Rebuilt, it became the home of the city police chief and in the early twentieth century was bought by Yeliseyev, owner of fabulous food emporia in Moscow and St Petersburg. After the Revolution until 1922, it became the Arts House, scene of literary evenings and heated debates, where Osip Mandelstam, among other poets and artists, found temporary shelter.

NEVSKY PROSPECT LOOKING DOWN TOWARDS THE ADMIRALTY BUILDING (*top*).

THE EQUESTRIAN STATUE OF PETER THE GREAT IN SENATE (DECEMBRISTS') SQUARE (*above*).

On the left bank of the Moika, which served as the city's main thoroughfare in the eighteenth century, stand many buildings that have significant associations in Russian history. It was on the first floor of No. 12 that Pushkin lived at the end of his life and the house is now a museum, where the poet's study is preserved, complete with his personal belongings, library and the couch on which he died after his mortal duel. On the Moika also lived the poet Kondaty Ryleyev, one of the five leaders of the Decembrist rising to be hanged, and here too is the Teachers Cultural Centre, former home of the Yusupov princes, where Rasputin was murdered in 1916.

Crossing the Moika, one comes to the Stroganov Palace, built by Rastrelli in baroque style in 1750–4, for Baron Stroganov, who had been granted the title by Peter I. This wealthy and powerful family of manufacturers, merchants and landowners are first mentioned in Russian chronicles in the fourteenth century and by the seventeenth century had established their renowned icon, embroidery and enamel-working studios. One of the halls in their ornate palace was devoted to a magnificent collection of paintings, which is now in the Hermitage museum.

Diagonally opposite, on the north side of the Nevsky Prospect and set back from it, is St Peter's Lutheran Church (now a swimming pool). It stands on the site of St Petersburg's first Protestant church, erected in the early eighteenth century: the city's first school was established under its auspices. The school, which produced many great Russian scholars and scientists, still exists and the ornamentation and latticework remaining on the first two floors recall the fashionable baroque style of the time.

The church stands back from the thoroughfare in a manner very characteristic of Nevsky Prospect, which acquired its distinctive look in the early nineteenth century when the canons of classicism and empire held sway. Monotony in the measured harmony of its architecture was avoided by unexpected breaks in the line of the buildings, so that stately churches or majestic palaces or serene little squares are set back from the street, providing charming changes of rhythm and 'drawing in' additional space.

Close to St Peter's Church, on the other side of the street, is a small, stately square formed by great colonnades curving out from the Cathedral of Our Lady of Kazan. Built in 1801–11 on the site of an early eighteenth-century wooden church, later rebuilt in stone as the biggest church in the city, the cathedral was commissioned by Paul I from the architect Andrei Voronikhin, who was charged with creating an even more majestic church, similar to St Peter

THE MEETING OF THE MOIKA RIVER AND THE FONTANKA CANAL.

THE SWEEPING COLONNADES OF THE CATHEDRAL OF OUR LADY OF KAZAN (*right*).

in Rome. Because the western side, where the main entrance would traditionally be, faced a narrow side-street, while broad Nevsky Prospect was on the north, the curving colonnades flanking the portico that forms the entrance were built on the north side. Voronikhin died before he was able to achieve his plan of adding another colonnade and square to the south, but his cathedral became a memorial to Russian military glory when the body of the Russian commander Mikhail Kutuzov, killed while pursuing the retreating French forces in 1813, was brought to St Petersburg for burial here. Later, statues of Kutuzov and Barclay de Tolly, also famed as a victor over the French, were installed in the square in front of the colonnades.

Just beyond the cathedral, Nevsky Prospect is intersected by a canal, from the bridge of which can be seen the Church of the Resurrection with its numerous cupolas and decorative mosaics. It was built on the spot where, in 1881, revolutionaries assassinated Alexander II, who twenty years earlier had finally abolished serfdom. In the early 1930s the church was temporarily a museum documentating the history of political imprisonment during the tsarist regime. It is now due to re-open as a museum of mosaic art.

Beyond the church is Adamini House, an austere three-storeyed building designed by Domenico Adamini in the 1820s, which became famous before the Revolution for the café in its cellar known as the Players' Stopping Place. Here, actors, artists and poets gathered.

Adamini House is on the corner of the land known as the Field of Mars. Originally known as the Tsarina Meadow, it acquired its name when towards the end of the eighteenth century it became the parade ground for reviews of the St Petersburg garrison and Guards. After the Revolution, at the suggestion of Maxim Gorky, those who had died in the fight to overthrow the monarchy were buried in the field. The memorial to them, designed by Lev Rudnev, consists of four massive stone monuments placed at the corners of a square in the centre of which burns an eternal flame; the monuments' epigraphs were written by the first Soviet Minister of Education, Anatoly Lunacharsky.

The western side of the Field of Mars is bordered by the former barracks of the Pavlov Regiment of Life Guards, while on the north is the Marble Palace, built by Rinaldi in 1768–72 for Grigory Orlov, a favourite of Catherine II. In severe neo-classical style, it was the first building in St Petersburg to have a stone and marble façade rather than the usual stucco facing. It is now The Lenin Museum.

The eastern boundary of the field is formed by the Swan Canal, which separates it from the Summer Garden, one of Peter I's favourite projects. The Tsar's Summer Palace, a

THE SUMMER PALACE OF PETER THE GREAT IN THE SUMMER GARDENS OVERLOOKING THE FONTANKA CANAL.

small two-storeyed house which was the first non-military stone structure to be built in St Petersburg, stands in the garden's north-eastern corner. Peter envisaged the Summer Garden not only as a place of relaxation and festivities but as a symbol of cultural enlightenment appropriate to his new Russia. Marble statues of classical gods and goddesses were brought from Italy and placed in the garden's avenues and glades, each with a tablet detailing the figure's mythological history. Pride of place was given to the ancient statue of Venus, purchased in Rome in 1719 and only brought to Russia after protracted negotiations over permission to export it; a wagon fitted with special springs was used to transport it over the last leg of the journey. Peter gave the pagan goddess of love and beauty a special gallery in the garden and, aware that putting a female nude on public display was a violation of all Russian tradition, had her guarded by sentries. At the end of the eighteenth century, the statue was moved to the new Tauride Palace, from which it got its name of the Tauride Venus. It is now in the Hermitage museum.

Continuing along Nevsky Prospect, by the entrance to the underground station is the Little Hall of the Leningrad Philharmonic, restored after bomb damage in the Second World War. It was formerly the home of Colonel Vasili Engelhardt and famed in the nineteenth century for its masked balls and musical evenings, attended by all of St Petersburg society, including the emperor and empress. The concerts featured some of Europe's most famous composers, among them Liszt, Berlioz and Wagner.

Nearby is St Catherine's Catholic Church, again set back from the buildings around it, and across the street the tower of the city Duma, which was erected in the nineteenth century to serve as an optical telegraph between the

Winter Palace and the monarch's summer residence in Tsarskoye Selo. Turning from Nevsky Prospect into Brodsky Street, the Hotel Europe is on our left and the Philharmonic Building (once the Noblemen's Assembly) opposite. Beyond the green square straight ahead rises the majestic, eight-columned portico of the Mikhailovski Palace, built in the early 1820s by Carlo Rossi for Grand Duke Mikhail, younger brother of Alexander I. The magnificence of the palace, set at the end of a large court-yard with a remarkable ironwork fence and bounded by low wings, quickly inspired admiration and King George IV of England, wanting to see its splendour, was sent a model of it and subsequently presented the architect with a medal.

Only the grand staircase, a few reception rooms and the Hall of White Columns, now called the Rossi Hall, have survived to give an idea of the original palace interior, where everything, including furniture and light fixtures, was designed by the architect. The rest of the palace underwent major changes at the end of the nineteenth century, when it was remodelled to accommodate the Russian Museum. It is now one of the largest museums of Russian art, ranging from the eleventh to twentieth centuries, and particularly famed for its collection of avant-garde art of the 1910s and 1920s which, despite strict prohibitions, was assiduously collected by the then dirctor of the museum, Vasili Pushkaryov. The square in front of the museum and Brodsky Street was executed in the same style as the palace and is now known as Arts Square. In the middle is a romantic, post-Revolutionary statue of Puskin by Anikushin.

ONE OF THE BAS-RELIEF SCULPTURES THAT DECORATE THE SUMMER PALACE (*top*).

THE MAGNIFICENT GILDED IRONWORK RAILINGS ON THE NEVA SIDE OF THE SUMMER GARDENS (*above and right*) WERE ERECTED IN 1784.

THE RUSSIAN MUSEUM: THE EXTERIOR
(*top and centre*).
THE ROSSI HALL (*above*).

THE MAIN STAIRCASE DESIGNED BY
CARLO ROSSI IN 1819 (*above*).

AN ICON DEPICTING ST GEORGE AND THE
DRAGON AND A SERIES OF SCENES FROM
HIS LIFE (*right*).

On the corner of Sadovaya Street and Nevsky Prospect are the Gostiny Dvor, Leningrad's main shopping arcade, built in the 1760s, and the State Public Library, the first of its kind in Russia and containing many valuable items, among them Voltaire's library. At the end of Sadovaya Street, on the south-east corner of the Field of Mars, is Mikhailovski Castle, built at the turn of the nineteenth century by the Italian architect Vincenzo Brenna for Paul I. Tormented by fears of plots against him, Paul had planned the castle, to contain within it a church dedicated to the Archangel Michael, and chosen the site, south of the Summer Garden. Brenna faithfully fulfilled his wishes, surrounding the castle with a deep moat and equipping it with cannon placements, spacious stables and two guardhouses. Ironically, however, in 1801 Paul I was brutally murdered in the castle by officers of the Guards and within hours of the assassination his son Alexander I moved out. Since then Mikhailovski Castle has housed only educational institutions, libraries and administrative offices. Dostoyevsky was the most famous student at the institution.

Further down Nevsky Prospect, at the corner of Malaya Sadovaya Street, is the splendidly ornamented grocery that once belonged to Yeliseyev – mentioned previously in connection with the Arts House. Built in the early twentieth century, it is a fine example of St Petersburg art nouveau. A short walk along Malaya Sadovaya Street brings us to Manège Square. At the beginning of the nineteenth century, when the moat around Mikhailovski Castle was filled in and a new road cut through the castle lands, many of the adjacent blocks and squares had to be rebuilt, among them this small square onto which the riding stables and drill hall backed. Rossi made the side wall of the stables the front of the building, decorating it with large pilasters and graceful mouldings; the riding school was turned into an indoor stadium 150 years later and given an appropriate entrance. On the end of the drill hall Rossi placed a loggia-style portico of two Doric columns and added an identical but purely decorative portico to the left of the stables.

This false portico sets the architectural tone for the vista that opens up from Nevsky Prospect. Standing before it looking towards the avenue, the picture is of a spacious square fronting the immense Alexandrinsky Theatre (now the Pushkin Drama Theatre) with its large loggia-style portico. Rossi's design resembled an enormous open-air theatre lobby; it was even paved with 'parquet', made of large, white-stone squares. The right side of the square is bounded by the austere Public Library, which has eighteen columns stretching along its façade, interspersed with many stone statues of philosophers and writers. A similar

THE MIKHAILOVSKI CASTLE (*left*).
ARCHITECT ROSSI STREET AND THE BACK OF THE ALEXANDRINSKY THEATRE (*overleaf*).

colonnade adorns the façade of the theatre, which forms the southern end of the square. On the eastern side Rossi placed two small, but majestic pavilions, adorned with statues of ancient Russian warriors. The view of the theatre and the sense of space created by Rossi were marred at the end of the eighteenth century when the ponderous monument to Catherine II was erected in the middle of the square. The work of Mikhail Mikeshin, it consists of a bronze figure of the Empress set on a base surrounded by statues of her illustrious retainers.

Behind the theatre is the beautiful Architect Rossi Street, named after its creator and remarkable for the sense of harmony created by the architectural rhythms of the two buildings that form its opposite sides, 22 metres (72 feet) apart. Paired Doric columns run the entire length of the second and third storeys of the two buildings, each 220 metres (720 feet) long. The building on the left is the home of the St Petersburg/Leningrad Ballet School.

Further down Nevsky Prospect one reaches the Fontanka Canal, the boundary of the city in Peter the Great's time, facing which are the main courtyard and graceful architecture of the Anichkov Palace, named after the first commander of the regiment which guarded the old town gates here. The palace was built in the 1740s for Empress Elizabeth's lover and morganatic husband, Count Alexei Razumovsky, and in the 1770s it became the home of another royal favourite, Catherine II's lover, Duke Grigory Potemkin. When in 1817 Alexander I decided to rebuild the palace for his brother, the future Nikolai I, he again commissioned Carlo Rossi. Nikolai was so enamoured of the interiors created by Rossi for the majestic building that he held the more intimate court balls here rather than at the Winter Palace and the monarch's office was subsequently moved to it. In October 1918 the Anichkov Palace was turned over to the City History Museum to house its valuable collections and archives, and today it is the city's Centre for Schoolchildren.

Both the palace and the bridge over the Fontanka, the first to be built into the city, are still called Anichkov. The original bridge was reconstructed in 1841, when the four bronze sculptures by Peter Klodt, depicting wild horses being broken in, were hoisted onto their massive granite pedestals at each side of the two ends of the bridge. The dramatic statues of the fiery horses and brave riders locked in struggle hold symbolic significance for the people of Leningrad and they were taken down and buried when the German bombardment of the city began in 1941, to be replaced in triumph once victory approached. Today only the deep scars in the bases recall the terrible shelling.

YELISEYEV'S ART-NOUVEAU GROCERY (*top*).
MIKESHIN'S STATUE OF CATHERINE THE GREAT IN FRONT OF THE
ALEXANDRINSKY THEATRE IN OSTROVSKY SQUARE (*above*).

On the other bank of the Fontanka, directly opposite the Anichkov Palace, is another palace, built in the mid-nineteenth century by Andrei Stackenschneider for an old diplomatic family, the Byeloselsky-Byelozersky. A dark-red building in pseudo-baroque style, it is similar to the Stroganov Palace on the bank of the Moika; the two palaces marked the extremes of Nevsky Prospect and were intended to complement each other. Perhaps an even clearer boundary line than the Fontanka is Liteiny Prospect, which intersects Nevsky Prospect a little further on, beyond which begins the area traditionally populated by minor civil servants. It was here in the crowded rented properties with well-like inner courtyards where the sun never shines, and tiny semi-basement shops, and further out in the residential districts surrounding the large factories, that ideas of social justice took root and brought the demand for urgent revolutionary change.

THE ANICHKOV PALACE AND THE ANICHKOV BRIDGE OVER THE FONTANKA (*above*).

ONE OF THE FOUR BRONZE SCULPTURES ON THE ANICHKOV BRIDGE BY PETER KLODT OF WILD HORSES BEING BROKEN (*top*).

THE BYELOSELSKY-BYELOSERSKY PALACE (*left*).
ONE OF PETER KLODT'S HORSE-BREAKER STATUES (*above*).

In 1917 the Bolsheviks established their headquarters in the Smolny Institute, an 'Educational Society for Young Ladies of Noble Birth' founded by Catherine II and built by Giacomo Quarenghi in 1806–8 on the the site of Peter the Great's tar – or *smola* – warehouses. In the mid-eighteenth century Peter's daughter, Empress Elizabeth, had commissioned Rastrelli to build a convent on another part of this site, to which she intended to retire. His slender cathedral, ornately decorated with groups of columns and assorted mouldings, culminates in five cupolas that rise 92 metres (302 feet) into the sky. It is flanked by equally ornate, two-storeyed dormitories built around a cruciform courtyard whose corners are emphasized by chapels with small, single cupolas. Elizabeth's death in 1762 marked the end of Russian baroque and sadly also meant the abandonment of the plan to complete the convent with an entrance marked by an immense arch topped by a bell tower.

Catherine II's school for noblewomen was originally housed in the dormitories of the intended convent, moving in 1808 to Quarenghi's new three-storeyed building alongside them. Shaped like a capital C, the Smolny Institute is in the restrained classical manner, its main entrance emphasized by a portico of eight columns. Here, on 7 November 1917, Lenin arrived, disguised as a workman, and from an office on the second floor he and Leon Trotsky directed the uprising that lead to the overthrow of Kerensky's government. Lenin announced the Revolution in the former school assembly hall in the south wing, where the Second All-Russian Soviet Congress of Workers, Soldiers and Peasant Deputies was being held.

In 1924 the square in front of the Smolny Institute was landscaped and a fence erected, with a temple-like gateway flanked by twin porticoes. The building, today the offices of the city's Communist Party committees, became the defence headquarters in the Second World War, when Leningrad endured a terrible 900-day German blockade. It began on 8 September 1941 when the last road linking Leningrad to the rest of the country was cut off and, under constant heavy bombardment with shells, incendiaries and bombs, the citizens – their numbers swelled by thousands of refugees from the surrounding towns and villages – were quickly also threatened with malnutrition, cold and disease. According to the official figures, by December 1941 alone 52,881 people had died of starvation. Incredibly, the city held out; to sustain morale, the theatres stayed open, lectures were given in the basement of the Hermitage and concerts held – on 9 August 1942 the city symphony orchestra performed Shostakovich's 7th Symphony at the Philharmonic Hall.

THE SMOLNY INSTITUTE.

The dead were buried in mass graves in the Piskarevskoye cemetery: on 20 February alone, 10,043 people were interred there and the final death toll ran into hundreds of thousands. The cemetery, which covers five hectares (12 acres), has become a monument to all those who perished in the blockade, and documents and photographs of that time are on display in the two pavilions near the entrance. The stone blocks that mark the mass graves are labelled with the years 1941, 1942 and 1943, and the cemetery is enclosed by a granite wall with reliefs depicting the city's defenders. A moving epitaph to the dead is written along it, and before the wall, standing on a high pedestal, is a majestic figure representing the Motherland.

The city for which so many died remains today elegant and graceful, particularly lovely viewed from the rivers or canals, looking up at the stately buildings with their porticoes, columns and bas-reliefs. The best place to say farewell to Leningrad is where it was born, on the spit of Vasilievsky Island, with a view of the spreading Neva, the imposing fortress, the Admiralty with its little golden ship floating over the city and the stately palaces of the tsars and princes. Today the western side of the island is Leningrad's 'front door' and in 1982 the elegant Port Terminal was erected on Naval Glory Square with, nearby, new residential buildings and the Primorskaya Hotel linked to the sea by a broad embankment, steps and terraces. The modern shoreline continues to fulfil Peter's dreams for his great harbour capital, a city that combines the squares and broad avenues of Paris, the ornate beauty of Venice and the commercial spirit of Amsterdam with a sense of the vastness of Russia.

THE RIVER NEVA AND THE PETER AND PAUL FORTRESS.

PETRODVORETS

(PETERHOF)

The magnificent palace of Peterhof – now known as Petrodvorets – was born alongside the rising city of St Petersburg. In the first years of the eighteenth century, when Peter the Great's new capital consisted of a few wooden houses near the fortress and harbour, it was still under threat of Swedish attack by King Charles XII. Russian troops armed with numerous artillery pieces protected St Petersburg from the north and west but to guard against possible attack from the sea a fortress was built on a small island called Kronstadt. The wooden fort with several dozen guns was constructed by court architect Domenico Tressini on the sand-bank between the island and the mainland, covering the passage to the River Neva.

Peter often visited the area to supervise the most important of the construction projects and a small wooden house was built near the fort where he could stay overnight, examine working-drawings and confer with his aides. Peter liked the place, which he named Peterhof, and in 1713 he commissioned the architect A. Schlueter to design a small summer palace there, using the Tsar's own sketches. Peter called it Monplaisir and building work began in 1714.

Stretching for 73 metres (240 feet) along the waterfront, Monplaisir is centred on a tall, austere, hall – the Gala Hall – 13 metres long, 7.5 metres wide and 8.5 metres high ($42^{1}/_{2} \times 24^{1}/_{2} \times 28$ feet), which is flanked by roofed, one-storeyed galleries. Abutting the galleries are two pavilions, known as Lusthouses or houses of entertainment, which have two-tiered roofs topped by small lantern towers. Adjoining the Gala Hall on the eastern side are the Lacquer Room, a kitchen – decorated in the Dutch style with coloured tiles and painted ceiling – and buffet room, and on the western side a secretarial room, the sovereign's bedroom and the Naval Study. In bad weather the Tsar could exercise indoors by walking from one pavilion to another, taking in the beauty of the rough seas or of the regular gardens south of the palace through the big gallery windows.

Two houses were erected in the gardens to accommodate guests and notices of the 'Rules', composed by Peter himself, were placed at the entrance. Whatever the rank of the guest, the rules were the same: to arrive at Peterhof by sea only; to obtain, before the meal, a card with the number of their bed; to sleep in that bed and nowhere else; to take

THE GILDED STATUE OF THE DISCUS THROWER ON THE GRAND CASCADE IN FRONT OF THE GREAT PALACE.

MONPLAISIR PALACE

nothing away from their beds, nor to borrow anything from another bed; and not to go to bed in boots.

In the mid-eighteenth century the guest-houses were expanded under the supervision of Rastrelli, Empress Elizabeth's leading court architect, who added a masquerade hall to the western house. (Masquerades were the favourite pastime of the Empress.) It was from this house in the summer of 1762 that Catherine II travelled in secrecy to St Petersburg to overthrow her husband Peter III and assume the throne. The house was subsequently known as Yekaterininsky.

Abutting the eastern house were the monarch's baths, a room for formal dinners in honour of holders of military orders, a kitchen and a room where special 'Order' services were held. The latter, restructured in the mid-eighteenth century, was decorated with tapestries featuring African scenes and renamed the Arapsky Room, from the Russian *arap*, meaning black servant.

The Monplaisir Palace was extensively damaged during the two-and-a-half-year German occupation of Peterhof in the Second World War and the lengthy restoration work has involved much effort, skill and expense. The biggest challenge was to restore the famous Lacquer or Chinese Room. The walls of this room were decorated with 73 papier mâché, lacquered plates of varying sizes, with exquisitely painted oriental scenes, in gold against a black background, depicting beautiful girls out for a stroll, men earnestly at work, birds of paradise fluttering in the air and exotic plants in full bloom. All the plates were made by Russian icon painters under the supervision of the German decorative craftsman, H. Brumkorst, and were placed in gilded frames or cartouches. In between the plates, on shelves decorated with patterns, stood fine examples of Chinese and Japanese ware.

Only three plates, one large and two small, were found in the ruins of the palace after the Second World War and,

THE FAÇADE OF THE GREAT PALACE, REDESIGNED BY RASTRELLI.

although even these were damaged by fire, artists from the village of Palekh were able to use them as guidelines to reconstruct the interior of the Lacquer Room. From the sixteenth century Palekh had been renowned for its icon painters and after the Revolution Palekh craftsmen had formed a co-operative to produce their beautifully decorated art. It took many years of arduous labour for the modern craftsmen of Palekh to recreate the exquisitely ornamented papier mâché plates and to restore the Lacquer Room so that it can be seen by visitors to Monplaisir today in its original grandeur.

The Monplaisir Palace was Peter I's private residence as well as his work place, which – like his office in St Petersburg's Winter Palace – no one was allowed to enter except by invitation of the monarch. Wishing to keep Monplaisir for moments of seclusion, Peter subsequently ordered the building of a large formal palace south of Monplaisir, sited on top of a ridge running along the seafront. Called the Upper Chambers, it was intended as a solemn monument to his victories over Sweden on land and at sea. The rows of windows were to open onto the sea and the gardens were to be filled with fountains, the constant play of their waters echoing the sound of the sea beyond. The great palace of Peterhof was to symbolize imperial power, through the taming of the waters.

Over 5000 men laboured on this grandiose project, although Peter, who died in 1725, did not live to see its culmination. It was under his daughter, the Empress Elizabeth, that the immense palace of Peterhof took its final shape. In 1746 she commissioned Rastrelli to renovate and expand Peter's palace, which he did by repeating the design of Monplaisir on a larger scale so that the smaller, lower palace and the great, upper palace were effectively linked. Galleries with formal pavilions at the end were added to both sides of the central structure, one crowned with a church dome and the other with an eagle (which came to be known as Under the Emblem). From every angle the eagle appears to be double-headed. The length of the palace was doubled, to almost 300 metres (1000 feet).

In the Great Palace, Rastrelli preserved Peter I's Oak Study, the Central or Italian Hall and the front staircase, which appears modest, too narrow and steep, for the new rooms which he decorated in sumptuous rococo style. Over the following reigns, each Russian ruler made his or her own additions and changes to the palace, and the only survivals from the mid-eighteenth century today are the Staatsdamsky Room, the Dance Hall and the Portrait Room. In the predominant style of the period, the latter is 'wall-papered' with pictures and has some 400 canvases by

both Russian and foreign painters, some of them of outstanding quality, others less so but always of historical interest. The interiors throughout Peterhof include many paintings, some of them brought here in 1925 from the storerooms of the Hermitage museum. In several cases, the paintings are by unknown artists and one anonymous work in the Portrait Room has proved of particular interest.

When restorers removed the sixteenth-century portrait of a young Italian woman from its frame, they discovered that the edge of the canvas had been bent over, concealing the name of the sitter: Vittoria Accoramboni. Her romantic life-story had become almost legendary over the centuries and she was the subject of a short story by Stendhal in 1837, published in his *Italian Chronicles*, and of the last novel, *Vittoria A.*, by the German writer Johann Tieck in 1840. She came from an old Urbino family and was renowned for her beauty, intellect and poetic talent. In 1573 she was married unhappily to the nephew of Cardinal Mantalto.

THE CROSS SURMOUNTING THE CHURCH DOME OF ONE OF THE TWO FORMAL PAVILIONS ADDED BY RASTRELLI TO THE CENTRAL STRUCTURE OF THE GREAT PALACE.

THE INTERIOR OF THE GREAT PALACE: THE GRAND BAROQUE
STAIRCASE (*top left*), THE HALL OF PICTURES (*centre*), AN OAK
PANEL IN PETER THE GREAT'S STUDY (*top right*).

PETER THE GREAT'S DESK IN HIS OAK STUDY (*above*).

who later became Pope Sixtus V. In 1581 he was killed by, it was rumoured, Vittoria's lover, Paolo Orsini, the Duke of Bracciano. An investigation of the murder failed to find proof but Pope Gregory XIII obtained a vow from the Duke that he would never marry Vittoria. Paolo at once broke the vow by marrying her in secret, but in 1585, when Pope Sixtus succeeded, the couple were forced to flee to Padua. Shortly afterwards Paolo died from a mysterious illness and a month later Vittoria was murdered.

Her portrait in Peterhof seems to show a cold, aloof woman with little of the beauty and passion associated with her. But fashions in beauty change, nor is the image-maker always to be believed. In a neighbouring room is a portrait of Catherine II, showing the Empress with the plump rosy cheeks and innocent blue eyes of a child, revealing no trace of the voluptuousness, cruelty, ambition and political intrigue for which she was so well known. It is, however, because of her that many of the palace interiors were splendidly redecorated.

No sooner had Catherine succeeded to the throne, in 1762, than she ordered two new Chinese rooms, differing greatly in their sumptuousness and extravagant décor from Peter's Lacquer Room in the Monplaisir Palace. Empress Elizabeth's ante-room was remodelled on Catherine's instructions to become a Room of Glory dedicated to the Russian navy. It was decorated with 12 paintings by J. Gakkert showing the victory of a Russian naval squadron over the Turkish armada in the Battle of Chesme, off the coast of Asia Minor, in 1770.

All Catherine's gala rooms, with their wealth of luxury fabrics, bronze, crystal, gilded carvings and plaster mouldings, were restored after 1945 according to surviving drawings and photographs. Before embarking on this painstaking restoration work, a model of the palace was constructed – just as was done 200 years before – in order to work out the details of the interior, which were barely discernible in the faded old photographs.

Wholesale restoration work had also to be carried out in the ruined palace gardens, from which the bronze and lead fountain sculptures had been removed by the Germans to melt down for munitions. Work on Peter's water park had first begun in 1716, when thousands of soldiers were assigned to dig a 24-kilometre (15 mile) canal, while foundry workers began to model numerous tritons, dolphins, naiads and other water figures in various shapes and sizes. (Bronze rather than the original lead was later used.) The main fountain featured a figure of Samson and the Lion, symbolizing the victory scored by the Russian hero over the Swedish lion in the war of 1700–21. The foundry work

BRONZE AND LEAD FOUNTAINS IN THE PARK (*top*).
THE CANAL LEADING TO THE BALTIC SEA (*above*).
SAMSON AT THE FOOT OF THE GREAT CASCADE (*overleaf*).

was not completed until 1735, ten years after Peter's death, and the statue seen today was installed in 1947, newly cast after the original had been taken away to Germany in the Second World War.

In front of the palace the canal opens into a semicircular lake with the figure of Samson placed on a rock at its centre; a powerful jet of water streams from the lion's mouth, while 22 more jets of water along the banks of the canal symbolize the faithful pages in the service of the hero. Rising behind Samson is the Great Cascade, which accompanies the visitors' passage up to the Great Palace. A powerful stone wall ornamented with gilded figures was built into the slope below the palace to create the cascade. Water streams over its seven giant steps and sword-like jets of water pierce the air from both sides of each step, which are flanked by bronze sculptures of Perseus, Actaeon, Pandora, Galatea and other heroes and gods of antiquity. An upper, shallow, grotto with seven arches is built into the middle of the wall, before which two jubilant tritons blow their horns, sending spurts of water all around. Below it is the great grotto, with marble statues displayed in its five deep niches. In front of it is a large water basket for water flowers, from the rim of which 28 jets of curving water flow downwards, feeding the lake with Samson as its centrepiece.

More than 40 statues and dozens of bas-reliefs and sculptural ornaments decorate the Great Cascade but, although it is the heart of Peterhof's water kingdom, it is by no means the only fountain complex. Altogether, in the lower and upper parks, there are 21 groups of fountains and cascades, ceremonious, playful, romantic and exotic. Each group has a minimum of eight or ten water-emitting devices which send forth numerous jets of water that may be in powerful or gentle streams, shooting straight up for many metres or curving through the air.

In May each year the Peterhof fountains resume their seasonal performance. In the evening, searchlights play on the flying streams of water while the sky above is lit by a glorious display of fireworks. Illuminated by flickering lights, with the background sound of cascading water, Peterhof then may seem at its most magically beautiful. But it is in the quiet of a weekday that it can be appreciated most, approached by sea as Peter the Great always did. Then the figure of Samson sparkles into view as the boat approaches the shore, with the great palace perched above, white and sky-blue, touched with gold. From there the wide, arrow-straight canal on which Peter used to sail his yacht leads to the palace, with its lovingly restored magnificent rooms and works of art.

DRAGON FOUNTAINS ON THE CHESSBOARD HILL CASCADE IN THE LOWER PARK.

PAVLOVSK

T he beautiful palace and park of Pavlovsk lies 27 kilometres (17 miles) from Leningrad on the Slavyanka river. In the eighteenth century this area was part of the crown's hunting grounds outside St Petersburg and in 1777 Empress Catherine II granted over 400 hectares (1000 acres) of land there to her son Paul and his wife Maria Feodorovna. This gift was not out of affection for Paul, for whom she had no love, but as an expression of her pleasure at the birth of her grandson, the future Tsar Alexander I. The young couple immediately had two small wooden houses built on the land: Marienthal – or Maria's Valley – and Paullust – Paul's Joy – but in 1780

Grand Prince Paul decided on the construction of a large palace. He commissioned the Scottish architect Charles Cameron, who had studied classical architecture in Rome and had arrived in Russia the previous year. Cameron's initial work as court architect to Catherine II was on the interiors of the Summer Palace at nearby Tsarkoye Selo.

Work on Paul's new palace began in 1782 and was completed in 1786. As soon as the foundation stone had been laid, Paul and Maria set off on a trip round Europe, travelling incognito as the Count and Countess Nord. Paul's artistic taste and devotion to music, the theatre and painting impressed European rulers that the couple met.

A STATUE OF TSAR PAUL I ON THE PARADE GROUND IN FRONT OF THE GREAT PALACE.

The building was in the Palladian style typical of the period and its majestic elegance seemed to fit the character of Paul as described by contemporary witnesses. The three-storeyed rectangular structure is crowned with a drum surrounded by 64 columns that support the weight of the large central dome, while curving wings flank this main structure, forming the front courtyard. The palace faces east, with the river behind, and is visible from afar.

Cameron's work on Pavlovsk was completed by the Italian architect Vincenzo Brenna and the late eighteenth-century interiors of Paul's Summer Palace remain today remarkably unchanged, a monument to late Russian classicism. The inside is divided into three parts. The front (east) entrance, on the ground floor, leads to the Egyptian Hall, designed by Cameron and which closely resembles Adam's great interiors. The northern suite of rooms to the right was used for informal occasions and comprised the French Room, the Dancing Hall, Parlour and Billiard Room. The huge mirrors that originally lined the Dancing Hall were replaced after Paul's death in 1801 with paintings by the French landscape artist Hubert Robert (1733–1808). The southern suite to the left, with bedroom, toilet room, study and Crimson Room, was used as Paul and Maria's private quarters; the study became the royal family's favourite room in which to spend their leisure evenings. Behind the Egyptian Hall lies the dining-room, overlooking the Slavyanka river valley.

The round Italian Hall, the heart of the palace's architectural composition, is on the first floor, above the dining-room. High-ceilinged and airy, it is illuminated by windows in the drum dome that crowns the palace. Behind it is the Greek Hall, a gem of classical design, its white walls setting off the columns of green artificial marble with magnificent Corinthian capitals.

The formal quarters of the Tsar and the Empress lie to the left and right of the two halls. Paul's suite begins with the War Hall, an octagonal parlour ornamented with bas-reliefs of armour and scenes of the Trojan War, and is followed by the Tapestry Room and a library and small study, separated only by an archway; a toilet room ends the suite. Maria Feodorovna's apartments also begin with a parlour, called in contrast the Hall of Peace and decorated with bas-reliefs of flowers, ears of corn, fruits and musical instruments. Next to it is her library, followed by the boudoir, with ornamental murals based on motifs used by Raphael in the loggias of the Vatican Palace. The formal bedchamber, with a huge bed under a magnificent canopy in the centre, is the most sumptuous room in the suite; beyond it is the customary toilet room.

A CERAMIC STOVE IN THE HALL OF PEACE (*top left*); AN IMPERIAL EAGLE IN THE HALL OF WAR (*top right*).
THE FOUR-POSTER BED IN THE FORMAL BEDROOM (*above*).

THE LIBRARY OF EMPRESS MARIA FEODOROVNA, HUNG WITH FRENCH GOBELIN TAPESTRIES.

The halls on the first floor of the palace's curved wings were also designed for formal use. They include the empress's library, off the landing of the front staircase, in which everything in the room – ornamentation, furniture, even book covers – was designed by Charles Rossi, Brenna's disciple. Maria later entrusted Rossi with the task of reshaping and decorating the palace at Yelagin where she spent the last part of her life.

In the palace's left wing is a spacious picture gallery and the formal dining-room. The interior decoration of the latter had been almost completed when Paul decided that the room should also serve as his throne room. Brenna, faced by this challenge, created niches in the corners where small stoves shaped as miniature ancient temples were installed and arches supported by caryatids were built between the niches and above the windows and doorways. Although significance was thus imparted to the room, the low ceiling deprived the large hall – 400 square metres (480 square yards) – of the gala appearance that was needed and Brenna commissioned the Italian decorative artist and architect P. Gonzaga to create a special *plafond*. Gonzaga's magnificent painted ceiling – a blue sky adorned with flags – created the illusion of height and space, and gave the room the festive atmosphere it had lacked.

A special wing was added behind the dining/throne room at the end of the eighteenth century to house the Knights' Hall, which was created by Paul specifically for assemblies of the Knights of Malta. The story of this order of knights had fired the imagination of Paul as a small boy when his tutor had read him tales of their chivalry and justice. The tutor's journal entry afterwards read: 'The Grand Prince imagined himself to be the Ambassador of Malta.' The knights' history went back to the time of the crusades, when the Order of the Knights of St John of Jerusalem had been formed. They had become known as the Knights of Malta in 1530, when the Holy Roman Emperor, Charles V, had given them the island of Malta, partly to secure an ally in his war with the Turks. In subsequent centuries, whenever Russia went to war with Turkey, as under Peter I and Catherine II, negotiations were opened with the knights.

With the French Revolution and Napoleonic wars, the knights were rooted out from Malta, which became French territory in 1798. They looked for shelter to other countries where they still had possessions, which included that part of Poland now annexed to Russia. When in January 1797 the knights' Polish prior, Count Litta, petitioned Paul for financial assistance, the Tsar promptly responded. He had ascended the throne only the year before, on Catherine II's death, and it seemed as if the opportunity to realize his boyhood dreams of establishing a special order of noble knights had now come. The 'Crowned Don Quixote', as Paul was sometimes known, gave the knights not only money but permission to set up a great priory in Russia, and he undertook to supervise the strict observance of the knights' laws and statutes.

In December 1798 Paul I was made head of the knightly Order at a solemn ceremony, in which he donned the symbols of his new rank – the gown, crown, sword and cross. He decreed that the official title of the Russian tsars should in future include the words 'Grand Master of the Order of St John of Jerusalem'.

The Knights' Hall at Pavlovsk was later used by Maria to display her collection of antique sculptures and burial urns, and is now the 'museum of antiques'. From it a passage leads into the palace church, though this unusual proximity of Oriental and Occidental churches did not concern Paul, whose overriding fear was of Jacobinism. In 1801 he even invited Pope Pius VII to settle in St Petersburg should the atheist French force him to leave Italy.

The Knights of the Order of St John did not last long in Russia after Paul's assassination in March 1801. Nor did Paul himself have much time to enjoy the palace he had created. It only became his favourite home after the death of Catherine II in 1796, perhaps because of its close proximity to Catherine's palace at Tsarskoye Selo. He spent only four summers at Pavlovsk, although the widowed Empress continued to live there until 1822. In her last years the journey became too tiring for her and she changed her favourite residence for the Yelagin palace on one of the islands of St Petersburg. After Maria's death in 1828, time seemed to stand still in Pavlovsk and the interiors, including furniture and many items of everyday life, have been almost miraculously preserved.

The gardens that surround the palace are also a remarkable tribute to eighteenth-century artistry. They were laid out at the same time as the construction of Pavlovsk and from the swampy and wooded area a beautiful park was created. Cameron's design was like a giant open-air interior, with small temples and pavilions, including the Temple of Friendship, the Apollo Colonnade, the obelisk in honour of the founding of Pavlovsk, and an open-air aviary called the Enclosure.

The vast park is divided into several gardens, each with its own character and becoming less formal, more broadly landscaped and nearer to nature as one moves from the palace towards the outskirts of the park. The formal garden around the palace was designed for entertainment and ornamental display, with features such as colonnades,

terraces with sculptures, water cascades and, beyond, picturesque ruins, a maze, follies and secluded arbours.

The next zone is known as the Old Forest or 'Old Sylvia', a memorial grove created to evoke remembrance of things past. Statues illustrating themes from antiquity are scattered through this portion of the park, with carefully laid out paths and a curved seat on the sloping river bank from which to contemplate the peaceful vista. 'New Sylvia' continues the lyrical mood. Nature here seems much closer, although the narrow, shaded paths are flanked by carefully trimmed shrubs and there are such features as the sculpture of Apollo, the Mausoleum and the End of the World column. Finally there is the White Birch area, an expanse of fields and meadows and inviting coppices which looks deceptively natural. But its straight paths lead to romantic vistas that have been shaped by man's imagination.

Pavlovsk's gardens are a magnificent example of Russian landscape art, on a par with the Villa d'Este or Versailles.

They are a place of enchantment, perhaps most beautiful in the early autumn, glowing with the changing colours of the leaves and perfumed by the lingering flowers.

In the Second World War the park was badly damaged; over 70,000 trees were cut down and shell-holes and trenches left ugly scars in the ground. For nearly three decades devoted gardeners worked to restore it; they removed the tree stumps and replaced them with new trees, planted over 90,000 bushes and shrubs, cleared the overgrown alleys and paths, and restored the man-made landscape. The glory of Pavlovsk came back to life.

The palace too suffered damage in the war and was lovingly restored, using old working-drawings, prints and photographs as guidelines. A small exhibit in the palace traces the restorers' painstaking, step-by-step work. Today Pavlovsk is not only a magnificent example of late eighteenth-century Russian classical architecture and landscape gardening but also a tribute to the art of restoration.

THE THRONE ROOM. THE TABLE IS SET WITH THE EIGHTEENTH-CENTURY SÈVRES ROSE SERVICE.

PUSHKIN
(TSARKOYE SELO)

This small town south of Leningrad was founded by Peter the Great and called Tsarskoye Selo – tsar's village – until the Revolution, after which it was first renamed Detskoe Selo, or children's village, and then in 1937, on the centenary of his death, Pushkin, in honour of Russia's national poet. The remarkable palaces built on the tsar's vast estate attracted many writers and poets, giving it a literary character unlike any of the other palace suburbs of Leningrad.

The town's origins go back to 1708, when Peter I presented a small homestead to his mistress and later second wife, Catherine, on the birth of their first child, the future Princess Anna. Ten years later a stone residence was built, to which the Tsar enjoyed paying unexpected visits

After the death of Peter in 1725 and of Catherine two years later, the house became the possession of their second daughter and only heir, Princess Elizabeth; her sister Anna had moved to Holstein on her marriage and had died there. During the reign of her aunt, Anna Ioanovna (1730–40), Elizabeth frequently sought refuge at Tsarskoye from the rages of the suspicious Empress and surviving documents show orders for rifles, gunpowder and bullets to be sent to her retreat.

When Elizabeth became empress in 1741 she decided to expand and enhance her patrimonial estate, and the commission was finally bestowed on Bartolomeo Rastrelli who had already won favour for his redesigning of the Peterhof palace. The huge Summer Palace at Tsarskoye Selo which he began building in 1749 is 325 metres (1066 feet) long and both the façade, with its decorative motifs and roofline, and the profusely ornamented interiors displayed the sumptuous rococo style, close to the late baroque architecture of central Europe in character. On seeing the splendid new palace, King Louis XV of France's envoy is said to have exclaimed to the Empress with flattering irony, 'What a pity that so magnificent a gem does not have a fitting case!'

The Tsarskoye palace was famous for its hanging garden, its giant ballroom with gilded carvings – 17 metres (56 feet) wide and an astonishing 47.5 (156 feet) metres long – and its breathtaking Amber Room. Rastrelli wrote proudly

THE CHURCH DOME OF THE SUMMER (CATHERINE) PALACE (*left*).　　THE FAÇADE OF THE SUMMER PALACE (*above*).

THE CAVALIERS' DINING ROOM (*top right and top left*) WHERE THE
EMPRESS DINED WITH CAVALIERS OF THE HIGHEST STATE ORDER.

THE HALL OF PICTURES (*above*).
A SUCCESSION OF GILDED DOORS (*right*).

decades the boxes containing the gift remained unopened in St Petersburg and it was only in 1755 that Elizabeth decided that she wanted it used at Tsarskoye Selo. Guards had to make the 30-kilometre (19 mile) journey carrying the valuable cargo by hand.

In the Second World War, the Germans dismantled the Amber Room and there were reports that the decorative treasures were on display in Königsberg, where an amber museum once existed, and also that the crates of amber were being stored in the caves of the local castle. According to another rumour the amber had been put aboard a ship which had been sunk while on its way to Germany and, later, there were claims that the amber was being kept somewhere in West Germany. In any event, the amber remains unlocated and the Amber Room remains the only unrestored room in the palace. An experimental workshop in Leningrad has been working for some years, studying old German books and documents to decode the secrets of tinting pieces of amber, with the aim of restoring the eighteenth-century interior.

The pleasure-loving Empress Elizabeth was fond of the Summer Palace at Tsarskoye Selo, where she came with her large court following and enjoyed the seasonal masquerades held here. Her German nephew and heir to the throne, the future Peter III, visited the palace eight times in seven years but at all times the Empress was surrounded by her numerous favourites and foreign envoys. Prussia in the mid-eighteenth century was a looming threat to Russia, a fact recognized by the extravagant, indolent but astute Elizabeth, and the palace and its grounds were a constant scene of political intriguing. England was angling to have Russia as a loyal ally and one confidential meeting that took place in the Hermitage Pavilion was between the Russian Vice-Chancellor Vorontsov and the British ambassador Dickens. The latter sent a message to London that £50,000 should be sent as a gift to Empress Elizabeth, who wished to add some embellishments to her palace; the Vice-Chancellor asked for only a few thousand pounds to help complete his mansion in St Petersburg.

Elizabeth's successor, Catherine II (1762–96), also fell in love with Tsarskoye Selo but, not finding the baroque and rococo styles to her taste, she decided to remodel the interiors. The Scottish architect Charles Cameron was appointed to supervise the work, which was begun in 1780 and carried out in the Adam style, new to Russia. Marble and sculptures were brought from Italy, precious wood for the parquet floors from India, unique samples of china from Saxony, China and Japan, and Lyons textiles from France. As well as restructuring the dining-room, bedrooms,

that, thanks to him, a large room in the palace was completely faced with white and yellow amber and all the piers decorated with amber bas-reliefs and other sculptured articles. This unique room was created in Berlin to designs by A. Schlueter: large wall panels were assembled from thousands of pieces of amber and rocaille amber frames set off relief images of classical goddesses, mirrors and illustrations of the 'five senses' executed in Florentine mosaics. The precious fossil resin had been presented to Peter I in 1717 by King Friedrich Wilhelm of Prussia but for several

THE BALLROOM OF THE SUMMER PALACE – RASTRELLI'S GREAT HALL (*top right and top left*).

THE FIGURE OF 'DAWN', ON THE UPPER LEVEL OF THE FRONT
STAIRCASE.

RASTRELLI'S GROTTO ON THE EAST SIDE OF THE LAKE (*top left*);
THE UPPER BATH PAVILION IN THE OLD GARDEN IN FRONT OF THE
PALACE (*top right*).

THE CAMERON GALLERY.

studies and front staircase, Cameron built exquisite court baths, with hot- and cold-water rooms. In 1784–5 he also added a special leisure pavilion and a gallery with an Ionic colonnade to the south-west wing of the palace; the walls of the pavilion, called the Agate Pavilion, were tiled with figured pieces of semi-precious agate and jasper.

Park pavilions and especially memorial structures were of particular concern to the ever-ambitious Empress. Interiors can always be remodelled by future generations but triumphal columns, arches, tombstones, would immortalize her reign. To mark recent Russian military and naval victories over Turkey, Catherine ordered four triumphal columns to be erected in the palace park: the Moreiskaya Column, commemorating the Battle of Moreya in October 1771; the Chesmenskaya Column, honouring the naval victory of June 1770; the Crimean Column, commemorating the seizure of the Crimea in 1783; and the Kagulaskaya Column, marking the routing by a 17,000-strong Russian army of 150,000 Turkish troops in the Crimea.

A memorial tower – now known as the Ruins – was also built in the park to commemorate the Turko-Russian war, which had been declared by Turkey in 1768 and ended in Turkey's overwhelming defeat at the hands of Russia in 1772. Not far from the Ruins are the Gatchina Gates of Triumph, modelled on similar triumphal gates in ancient Rome and commemorating the successful action by Count Grigory Orlov, Catherine's lover, during an outbreak of plague in Moscow in 1771. More personal monuments include the tomb of her particular favourite, Count Lanskoi, who died aged 30 in 1784, of exhaustion, and that of her beloved dog Zemira, for whom the epitaph was written by the French ambassador, Count Ségure.

ONE OF THE GILDED PARK GATES NEAR THE LYCEUM.

No other Russian ruler glorified his or her reign with memorial structures as much as Catherine. Alexander I (1801–25) was to build an impressive Arch of Triumph to commemorate the victory over Napoleon and Nikolai I (1825–55) was to erect a monument to commemorate the war with Turkey of 1828–29 (which looks strangely like a mosque), but they cannot compare with Catherine's remarkable building activity.

In 1792 the Empress commissioned Giacomo Quarenghi to build yet another palace at Tsarskoye Selo, called the Alexandrovsky Palace. It was a mark of Catherine's wish that her grandson Alexander should directly inherit the throne, bypassing her unloved son, Paul, whose brief reign would end in his assassination in 1801. Quarenghi's neoclassical building was of exquisite elegance, accentuated by a solemn double colonnade joining the two wings.

In 1811, ten years after Alexander had become tsar, he set up a lyceum at Tsarkoye Selo, which at first occupied a wing added to the church of the Summer Palace. This institution of higher learning was to train selected youths of noble families for important government positions and among the first 28 boys chosen to study there were the future foreign minister Alexander Gorchakov, the military officers involved in the Decembrist revolt, Ivan Pushchin and Wilhelm Kuehelbekker, and the admiral, Fyodor Matyushkin (who was to command the Sveaborg fortress in the Baltic in the summer of 1855, when an English naval force bombarded it for 45 hours to no avail). Another of the first students was Modest Korf, who went on to become the official historian of the reign of Nikolai I. The most distinguished early pupil of all, however, was Russia's national poet Alexander Pushkin, who after his studies at the Lyceum joined the government service in 1817, only to be exiled in 1820 for his liberal ideas.

It seems that the palaces and parks of Tsarkoye Selo have a special atmosphere, an enchantment that inspired Pushkin and has since inspired many other poets. Pushkin admitted that it was at Tsarskoye Selo that the muse of poetry first visited him, when as an adolescent he 'willingly read Apuleius and did not read Cicero'. Among the other great Russian poets who came here are Derzhavin, Zhukovsky, Krylov, Vyazemsky, Tyuchev, Annensky, Akhmatova, Gumilev and Mandelstam. The spirit that drew them there is captured by Mandelstam, St Petersburg's supreme poet, when he wrote, 'Let us go to Tsarskoye Selo and be free, frivolous and fervent.'

Mandelstam was born in 1892, two years before Russia's last monarch, Nikolai II, ascended the throne, with a court that was recorded in 1912 as having a staff totalling 1220 people, including 37 masters of ceremony and 42 doctors of medicine. Nikolai's favourite residence became the Alexandrovsky Palace and it was here, after his abdication on 2 March 1917, that he and his family lived under house arrest until August, when they were taken to Tobulsk and later Ekaterinburg, where in July 1918 they were executed.

Just over two decades later Tsarkoye Selo was devastated by the Germans before their retreat in the Second World War. Its great palaces, monuments and parks have been gradually restored in recent years and the place that so many Russian monarchs loved and favoured, and has attracted so many poets and writers, continues to exert its charms. In the 1920s the Russian art critic E. Gollerbach called it a 'town of the Muses' and his description still holds true of the spirit of Tsarkoye Selo, aptly renamed after the poet who first found inspiration there.

A STATUE OF PUSHKIN IN THE GARDEN OF THE OLD TSARSKOYE SELO LYCEUM WHERE HE STUDIED.

THE BLACK SEA

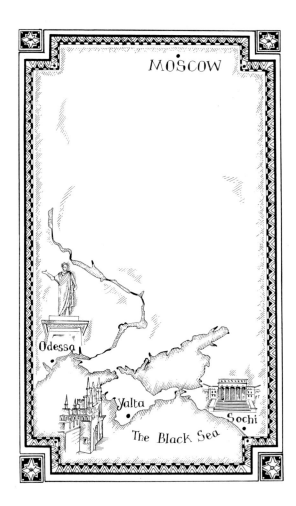

THE SEABOARD PROMENADE ON
THE BLACK SEA AT YALTA
IN THE CRIMEA.

For centuries this huge inland sea, linked with the Sea of Azov to the north-east and with the Mediterranean through the Dardanelles to the south-west, was the scene of military clashes and diplomatic manoeuvres. The ancient Greeks ventured into its vast expanses, in search of the grain of the Crimea and the legendary Golden Fleece of Colchis. Then the low-lying ships of the great Byzantine Empire ploughed its waters in all directions. From the Empire's capital of Constantinople, Byzantine culture and Christian civilization were brought to Kiev and the old Russian cities. After the Empire began to crumble in the eleventh century, the swift caravels of the Genoese merchants sailed the Black Sea, loaded with grain and slaves from the Crimea. Finally, in 1453, the Turks captured Constantinople and the Black Sea was sealed off from the Christian world.

The early Russian sovereigns were well aware that their landlocked country had few prospects. In the sixteenth century Ivan the Terrible made an unsuccessful attempt to win a stretch of the Baltic coast for his Muscovy Empire and a century later Tsar Alexei Romanov turned his gaze southwards to the Black Sea but did not have the mettle to start a war with the Turks. His daughter Sophia twice sent Russian troops to the Sea of Azov coast and both times had to withdraw them ingloriously.

The young Peter the Great in his turn twice marched to the Sea of Azov, in 1695 and 1696, and at the cost of tens of thousands of Russian lives finally captured the fortress of Azov at the mouth of the Don, giving access to the sea. The Black Sea itself, however, still remained closed and in 1710–11, emboldened by his successes on the Baltic, Peter went to war with Turkey. Overwhelmed by Turkish troops on the River Prut, he was forced to barter his wife's jewellery to preserve his army. He also had to give up Azov.

The dream of the Black Sea, however, had become deeply rooted in the minds of Russia's rulers. In 1735, under Empress Anna, Russia again went to war with the Turks, but after three years and the loss of some 100,000 lives an inconclusive peace treaty was signed with no gains, other than regaining Azov, for Russia.

It was Catherine the Great who brought the efforts of her predecessors to a brilliant finale. No sooner had she declared war on Turkey in 1769 than she despatched a large Russian flotilla to sail westwards around Europe and into the Mediterranean, while the Russian army marched south to the Black Sea, capturing the Crimea and advancing across the Danube on the sea's western shores. The sight of the Russian fleet in close proximity to Constantinople, just as the victorious Russian army was also nearing their capital, paralysed the Turks. The governments of Europe flew into a panic at the prospect of a strong Russia on Europe's southern flank and a peace was engineered. Catherine the Great gained the Crimea, with free access to the Black Sea, and hapless Turkey was saved.

Further wars and diplomatic moves followed and, although any significant Russian victory was generally negated by the European powers, by the mid-nineteenth century Russia had the northern and eastern shores of the Black Sea under its control. The three important towns of Yalta, Odessa and Sochi began to grow.

A BOAT NEAR SAIL ROCK OFF THE WINDING CRIMEAN COAST.

YALTA

This small town on the south-eastern coast of the Crimean peninsula, part of the Ukraine region, is now the centre of the Crimea's holiday resort area, with the attractions of a mild climate and the waters of the Black Sea set off by the rising mountains behind. In Russian minds its name is inextricably linked with the writer Anton Chekhov, who came to live here in the late 1890s.

There have been settlements in Yalta since time immemorial. In the fifth century B.C., when Pericles ruled Athens, the Greeks established a small colony here called Yalita and variations of the name were used by those who came later. When the Crusaders marched on the Orient in the Middle Ages, the place came into the hands of the Genoese, who built a small fortress called Gialita, later captured by the Turks and named Jalita. In 1783 Russia won the Crimea from the Turks and the name Yalta appeared for the first time on maps of the Russian Empire. At that time there were only eighteen houses there.

Half a century later, in 1838, the Governor-General of the Ukraine and Moldavia, Prince Mikhail Vorontsov, granted Yalta its town charter. Prince Mikhail was an exceptional figure: he had been educated in London, where his father was the Russian ambassador, and had joined the Russian army in 1803, winning renown for his bravery and military leadership during the 1812 war against Napoleon. As Governor-General of southern Russia he did much to revive the vine-growing and wine-making that had thrived there under the Greeks.

When the royal family appropriated a large tract of land to the west of the town, about 300 hectares (740 acres) in all, Yalta immediately became popular. The mild climate, light rainfall and abundance of sunshine particularly attracted the sick and convalescent, and towards the end of the nineteenth century Yalta had about 10,000 permanent residents, while at least twice that number of people came each year simply to enjoy themselves. Chekhov pointed,

not without irony, to the 'two most noticeable features of the smart Yalta crowd: middle-aged ladies dressed like young women, and a great many generals...'.

Because of his tuberculosis, the writer himself came to the town to avoid the damp springs and autumns of Moscow and St Petersburg, and in 1898 he decided to build a

THE ELABORATE MOORISH SOUTHERN FAÇADE OF THE VORONTSOV PALACE AT ALUPKA, BUILT BETWEEN 1828 AND 1846 FOR PRINCE MIKHAIL VORONTSOV.

house there. An impractical man, he was led into paying too much for a poor patch of land in the Tartar village of Autka, north of Yalta, on a mountain slope next to a Muslim cemetery. To make a garden from this hilly, barren site was to take the persistent efforts of Chekhov and his family over the next few years.

In 1899 the house was ready to live in and, having sold his estate outside Moscow, Chekhov moved in with his mother and sister Maria. His thin, tall and slightly stooping figure soon became a familiar sight in Yalta. Chekhov's numerous letters, tinged with sadness and irony, tell of his new life and the cheerful atmosphere during visits by fellow-writers, who included Ivan Bunin, Vladimir Korolenko and Maxim Gorky. In 1900, the Moscow Art Theatre company came to Yalta and its founders, Stanislavsky and Nemirovich-Danchenko, paid a surprise visit to their terminally ill friend. The company's tour was remembered for many years and the building where they performed

has miraculously survived subsequent wars and periodic frenzied bouts of reconstruction activity.

During the few remaining years of Chekhov's life – he died in 1904 aged only forty-four – he worked feverishly in his house at Yalta, overlooking the sea far below. Here he wrote his plays *The Three Sisters* (1901) and *The Cherry Orchard* (1904), masterpieces that were produced by the Moscow Art Theatre, and several short stories, among them the brilliant 'In the Ravine', 'The Bride' and 'The Bishop'. After his death his sister preserved the house exactly as it was in Chekhov's lifetime and in 1926 she was appointed director of the Chekhov Museum that was set up there. During the grim 30-month German occupation in the Second World War, when a German major was billeted there, she used her tact to protect the Museum from looting and she continued her guardianship right up to her death in 1954 – at the age of ninety-three.

Little today remains of the Yalta of Chekhov's time, which suffered from a terrible earthquake in June 1927, followed by the destruction of the Second World War when Soviet troops retreated from the Crimea in 1941 and recaptured the peninsula in spring 1944. The lively city now has a population of 85,000, a number swelled many times over in the summer and autumn when visitors come to stay in the hotels and sanatoria that dot the coastline. (In 1900 Chekhov was delighted to have organized a small guest-house for TB sufferers.) In the evenings the seaboard promenade, stretching for several kilometres on either side of the town, is filled with people out for a stroll, enjoying the sea air, watching the ships and listening to music.

CHEKHOV'S HOUSE IN YALTA.

THE GOTHIC BUILDING OF SWALLOW'S NEST, PERCHED ON THE OVEHANGING CLIFF OF CAPE-AI-TODOR (*above*).
A CANOPIED BALCONY IN THE OLD TOWN OF YALTA (*right*).

THE LIVADIA PALACE: CONFERENCE HALL
(*top*), THE INTERIOR (*centre*), THE
CENTRAL COURTYARD (*above*).

THE LIVADIA PALACE.

Along the coast to the west of the town centre is Livadia, the royal enclave that helped make Yalta so popular in the last century. Here Alexander III had a summer palace built for him, designed by Monighetti, and it was here, in a small, low-ceilinged room of which the tall, powerfully built Emperor was particularly fond, that he died in 1894. The present white palace, standing in a magnificent park famous for its 1000-year-old oak, is a rebuilding by Krasnov for Nikolai II in 1910–11. This was where the Yalta Conference of the Allies was held in February 1945, when Churchill, Roosevelt and Stalin discussed the future of Europe after Germany's imminent defeat and reached agreement on setting up the United Nations Organization. The palace is now a sanatorium but in the spacious hall is still the round table at which the Allied leaders convened.

Eastwards along the coast is the wine-making centre of Massandra, famous for its portwine. Established for over 150 years, it relies both on time-proven, traditional methods as well as the latest scientific techniques – it has its own research centre – to produce its fine fortified wines. Also not far from the town centre are the medieval Armenian church and the palace of the Emir of Bukhara, built in 1903 in Moorish style.

Moving further from Yalta, there are the beautiful mountains and valleys of the Crimea to be explored. The new road out to the airport passes the Uchan-su waterfall, an almost 100-metre (300 feet) drop and awesome after heavy rains, while further on, the north-eastern fringe of the Ai-Petri plateau is dotted with numerous caves, some of them believed to be as deep as 400 metres (1280 feet). Most picturesque of all is the route through the Belbek valley, where traces of mesolithic settlements dot the steep mountain slopes, and overhanging rocks line the narrow gorge called the Belbek Gate. About 40 kilometres (25 miles) to the north lies Bakhchisarai, the City of Gardens, which for many centuries was the capital of the Crimean khans; here are old monasteries and temples, and the palace, now a museum, once praised by poets.

THE BOTANIC GARDENS AT MASSANDRA WITH THE MAGNIFICENT BACKDROP OF THE MOUNTAINS OF THE CRIMEA.

ODESSA

The largest merchant port in southern Russia, Odessa lies on a bay in the north-west corner of the Black Sea, between the Dnieper and the Dniester estuaries. It was founded by Catherine the Great in 1794, on the site of the ancient Greek colony of Odessos – evidence of Odessa's thriving early past is shown in the city's Archaeological Museum. The Greek colony was wiped out by the Huns as they swept westwards in the third and fourth centuries, and eleven centuries passed before people came to live here again. The trading town of Kachibei sprang up first, and was later turned by the Turks into the powerful fortress, Khajibei.

In 1789 the Turks' reputedly impregnable stronghold fell to a Russian naval force under Captain Joseph de Ribas

THE 192 RICHELIEU STEPS LEADING DOWN TO THE PORT FROM THE SEAFRONT TERRACE (*left*).

SHIPS IN THE PORT OF ODESSA (*left and above*).

after a bombardment lasting less than 30 minutes; Akhmet-Pasha, the Turkish commander-in-chief, proved the main prize. De Ribas, a Catalan nobleman, had been a second lieutenant in the Neapolitan Guards when invited to Russia by Catherine the Great's favourite, Alexei Orlov. They had met after Catherine had despatched Orlov to Europe in the 1760s to locate a woman calling herself Princess Tarakanova, who said she was the natural daughter of the late Russian Empress Elizabeth. On his travels Orlov had come across de Ribas and been attracted by his energy and wit. He also successfully tracked down the 'princess', who supposedly fell in love with him at first sight, and the two were married. Accompanied by de Ribas, the couple travelled back to Russia – where the unfortunate woman ended her days a prisoner in St Petersburg's Peter and Paul Fortress.

De Ribas, however, won the Empress's favour by distinguishing himself in Russian service. He proved his courage and military skill when, under the command of Suvorov, he took part in the storming of Izmail, another Turkish fortress on the Danube – a picturesque account of which is given by Byron in *Don Juan*. Shortly afterwards, in 1794, the indefatigable de Ribas put forward the idea of converting Khajibei into a Russian naval base. Catherine's new town and port, bearing the ancient name of Odessa, was just established when de Ribas died in 1800. The central street in Odessa, named after him, is as renowned as Kreshchatik in Kiev or Nevsky Prospect in St Petersburg.

At this time, following the French Revolution, Catherine the Great willingly accepted supporters of the French *ancien régime* into Russian service and it was Armand Emmanuel du Plessis, Duc de Richelieu, who in 1803 was appointed the first Governor-General of Odessa and the entire northern Black Sea coast, then called 'New Russia'. A descendant of the famous Cardinal Richelieu of King Louis XIII's reign, the Duke – as the Odessans simply refer to him – did much to develop the port during his twelve years in office. Ordinary houses began to be built of the local yellow 'shell' limestone and the intensive quarrying that continued over the next century left a vast, entangled network of catacombs under the city, like those in Rome. During the Second World War they gave shelter to partisan detachments which the occupying German and Rumanian forces were unable to dislodge.

In 1815 the Duc de Richelieu returned to France, where he was appointed first minister in Louis XVIII's cabinet. A statue of him, made in 1828 by the celebrated Russian sculptor Ivan Martos, was erected in Odessa on the topmost landing of the flight of 192 steps leading down to the sea. The Odessa steps are immortalized in Sergei Eisenstein's classic film, *The Battleship Potemkin*, based on the 1905 mutiny at Odessa: in the film's most famous sequence, a frenzied piece of cross-cutting alternating between close-ups and panning shots, the boots of the soldiers are seen marching inexorably down the steps, driving the mutinous sailors and workers back to the port, innocent civilians are mown down by soldiers' fire as they retreat down the steps, a lone pram released by a mortally wounded woman, bumping dangerously ahead of them.

SOME OF THE OLD HOUSES OF ODESSA
PAINTED WITH CHARACTERISTICALLY
BRIGHT COLOURS (*above and centre*).

THE COLUMNS OF THE TOWN HALL

The new port attracted bold and enterprising people of all nationalities and Odessa became a lively mix of Greeks, Italians, Jews and Russians, all contributing their specific brand of humour. Odessa is still famed for its jokes and, appropriately, the town is now the venue for an international festival of comedy films, at which the winning entry is awarded with a small copy of the Duke's statue.

The Duke was succeeded by a fellow-Frenchman, General Langeron, and under his governorship Odessa became a free port in 1817, encircled by a deep moat spanned by several bridges, each with its own customs post. To honour Langeron's achievements, one of the central streets (today Lastochkin Street) was named after him. Odessa's heyday was under the third Governor-General, the Russian Anglophile Mikhail Vorontsov, in the years up to the mid-nineteenth century, by which time the flourishing city rivalled the other large centres of the Russian Empire, coming fourth after St Petersburg, Moscow and Warsaw in wealth and population. A passenger steamship line was set up and the first newspaper, in both Russian and French, started publication in 1827.

Many of Odessa's architectural features date to Vorontsov's period of governorship: the famous steps, the Governor-General's palace (now the Palace of Young Pioneers), the Stock Exchange (rebuilt and now the City Council) and Naryshkina's palace (now the Sailors' Cultural Centre). Three years before he died in Odessa in 1856, a monument was erected by the city to Vorontsov.

Although free port status had been abolished in 1849, Odessa continued to thrive. Its turnover was comparable to that of St Petersburg, Russia's main port, and banking – and smuggling – flourished. The *nouveaux riches* displayed their wealth by beautifying Odessa: the new Stock Exchange (1889) and the Opera House (1887) were intended to surpass their European counterparts in splendour – particularly those in Vienna. Nothing was too good for Odessa: if a touring opera company was invited, it had to be the best that Italy could offer.

In this wealthy city jewellery was very much in vogue and jewellers did a brisk trade. One of the most crafty of them, Rukhomovsky, caused an uproar among art connoisseurs in Europe when in 1896 he offered the Vienna Museum what he claimed to be a golden tiara of the Scythian king, Saitafern, supposedly found among the ruins of the ancient Greek city of Olbia. The Museum was saved from buying a fake only because of the prohibitive price demanded, but the tiara – after experts had declared it genuine – was then bought in France for 200,000 francs. In 1903 the truth came out in a Paris newspaper and Rukhomovsky,

the real creator of the 'masterpiece', was invited to France. The tiara was transferred from the Louvre to the Museum of Decorative Art, though it was soon returned to the Louvre, to be hidden away in one of the vaults. It is perhaps typical of the Odessan approach to life that the reaction of the city's journalists was to ridicule the gullible art specialists for their foolishness.

In the Revolutionary years of the 1910s and 1920s, a group of original young writers and poets emerged in Odessa, including Isaak Babel and Yuri Olesha, whose early, ironic works are now considered classics of Soviet literature. After the city's sufferings in the Second World War, Odessa became a rather grimmer city and the exodus of the 1970s transferred much of Odessa's distinctive humour to New York – where there is now a 'Little Odessa' on Brighton Beach. But the satirical tradition has not totally disappeared and some of the best Soviet satirical writers today are natives of this sunny, friendly city with its fine harbour and splendid old streets.

THE GRAND STAIRCASE OF THE OPERA HOUSE.

SOCHI

The jewel of the Black Sea's eastern coast, Sochi is an extremely popular holiday resort. It grew up as a health centre in the nineteenth and twentieth centuries, on the site of an old fort, and today Greater Sochi extends along 140 kilometres (87 miles) of the coast, from Lazarevsky in the north to Adler in the south, engulfing several smaller towns, including Dagomys, famed for its tea plantations, which now regularly hosts international conferences.

The long-destroyed Navaginsky fort from which Sochi developed was built in the late 1820s as one of 17 forts along the north-eastern Black Sea coast, from Azov in the west to

HOLIDAY-MAKERS SUNBATHING AND WINDSURFING ON THE BEACH AT SOCHI.

A WORKING CHURCH IN THE RESORT OF DAGOMYS.

Batumi at the south-eastern end of the Caucasian peninsula. The Caucasus was, and still is, a wild area of mountain and plateau, with the great Caucasus mountain ranges running from the Black Sea through to the Caspian Sea, the south of which borders present-day Iran. This region was brought within the control of the Russian Empire in the first half of the nineteenth century. Already, in the late eighteenth century, Georgia, a cluster of small principalities south of modern Sochi, had voluntarily joined with Russia and in 1827 the Georgian nobility were granted the same rights as their Russian counterparts. At the same time the petty khanates along the Caspian coast of the Caucasus (now Azerbaijan) were subdued by force and incorporated into the Russian Empire, followed by eastern Armenia in 1828, under the Turkmanchai Treaty that ended the 1826–28 war with Persia. Only the tribesmen of the North Caucasus and Black Sea coast around present-day Sochi refused to submit to Russian control.

It was General Paskevich, sent in 1827 to command the Russian army in the Caucasus, who ordered a chain of forts to be built along this part of the coast. He was the replacement for General Yermolov, a hero of the 1812 war and an attractive figure with a large popular following, who had been dismissed by Nikolai I. After the Decembrist uprising of 1825 the Emperor was fearful of the General's popularity – there was even talk that Yermolov might separate the Caucasus from Russia and form his own state.

The coastal forts were intended to prevent ammunition from the Turks and the British – both apprehensive of Russia's presence in Transcaucasia – reaching the rebel hillsmen. An article in the London *Morning Chronicle* of 1837 described a meeting on the coast between the reporter, a British arms-supplier named Bell 'and a large gathering of the hill clans during which the clans were promised further British aid. In 1839 Bell returned to incite the hillsmen to attack the Navaginsky fort.

Fighting, however, was not the main problem faced by the soldiers in the forts, for whom life was frequently a veritable hell. Communications with Russia were only possible by sea, and in the winter months when navigation ceased, the long nights set in, with drenching rain and terrifying storms; those who could afford it frequently drank themselves into a stupor. Many died from fevers and intestinal disorders, which took a far heavier toll than enemy bullets. In 1845 alone, 2,427 people died from various illnesses and only 18 from fighting.

Finally, in 1854, it was decided to destroy the line of fortifications and the forts were blown up. From 1866 onwards settlers from Russia, and even from as far away as Poland and Estonia, began to flock to the new region, attracted by land and money loans. The Dakhovsky customs post took the place of the Navaginsky fort and the new settlement of Sochi – a name derived from the nearby river – grew up around it. By 1900 there were 1,309 people living in Sochi and it boasted its own church, a hospital with eight beds and no less than 55 small shops and stores.

The fame of Sochi began to spread in the early 1900s because of the warm sulphurous springs in the Matsesta valley where the settlement was located. The healing properties of the springs had long been recognized by the local

A WOODEN PLANTATION HOUSE IN THE TEA-PRODUCING DISTRICT AROUND DAGOMYS.

A SAMOVAR POSITIONED AT THE DOOR OF ONE OF THE PLANTATION HOUSES (*above*).
TEA GROWING ON THE HILLS AROUND DAGOMYS (*overleaf*).

architecture. The 1931 Defence Commissariat sanatorium is built within the then permitted limits of constructivism, while the Pravda (1936) and Ordzhonikidze (1937) sanatoria are in the universally obligatory pseudo-classical style. This same period style also shows in several houses built at that time along the coast for members of the government, one of them intended for Stalin; all of them seem like displaced classical temples.

The subsequent pseudo-Empire style, a natural response to victory in the Second World War (and after Stalin's death in 1953 jokingly referred to as the 'Vampire' style), is exemplified by the railway station (1951) and the 'Metallurg' sanatorium (1956). They are both the work of Alexei Bushkin, who designed two of Moscow's most elegant underground stations – Kropotkinskaya and Mayakovskaya, but here seems to have been infected by the spirit of bureaucratic pomposity.

Sochi, along with many another city, did not escape the effects of Krushchev's campaign in the 1950s against 'excesses' in architecture in the rush to fill housing needs, which resulted in the mushrooming of ugly, reinforced concrete apartment blocks and barrack-style public buildings. Only in the late 1970s and early 1980s did attractive contemporary buildings begin to appear in Sochi, thanks to a growing interest first in post-modernist and then in post-constructivist styles of architecture.

Today, the resort area of Sochi is filled with hundreds of sanatoria, rest-homes and hotels, with an annual influx of up to two million people. They come from all over the country – Kamchatka in the far East, the Pamir mountains of Central Asia, Norilsk beyond the Arctic Circle, the farmlands of the Ukraine – arriving by train, plane or sea; the sea passengers come in at the passenger port built in 1935 which imitates the towers of the Moscow Kremlin with its spire and ruby star.

They are drawn by the bright sun and gentle waters, and the scented air from the light sea and mountain breezes. From the top of Bytkha mountain, the town can be seen stretched out along the coast far below, while nearby a winding road leads up the Agura valley, where the sulphur springs bubble up in the grottoes and caves. Past the impressive Eagle Cliffs is the Agura waterfall, a drop of 27 metres, (89 feet) and from here the road climbs to the Bolshoi Akhun summit, topped by a pseudo-Romanesque folly, a 30-metre (100 feet) tower built in 1936. Its top-floor restaurant, 663 metres (2175 feet) above sea-level, gives a panoramic view of the coast, the great Caucasian mountain range, dark-green forests and alpine meadows. Sochi indeed seems a paradise on earth.

people, who bathed there to help cure skin diseases and treat heart conditions, but in 1902 an enterprising man installed two wooden baths and spread the news of the miraculous qualities of the local water. Sick people began to come to Sochi and in 1909 a much needed hotel was built, followed by a bath-house the next year. Gradually Sochi was transformed into a flourishing spa town.

The railway line finally built along the coast reached Sochi in 1925, after which the town rapidly became a health resort for trade union and other organizations. Sanatoria sprang up along the main street, with the military the first to build there, closely followed by heavy industrial enterprises; the Soviet publishers, Pravda, the Commissariat of Internal Affairs and the Academy of Sciences were among many others to follow suit. Sochi became a showcase of Soviet architecture, with buildings by all the major architects of the time: the Vesnin brothers, Zholtovsky, Shchusev (who built Lenin's Mausoleum), Kolli and others.

A stroll down Sochi's main street, Kurortny (or Health Resort) Prospect shows the successive styles in Soviet

THE SPA AND BATHING ESTABLISHMENT IN MASESTA, A RESORT EAST OF SOCHI.

THE INTERIOR OF THE PASSENGER PORT.

INDEX